We live in the greatest hour of history. God is moving in the nations of the earth in an unprecedented way. At the same time, a generation is yearning to know their purpose. You are a crucial part of God's plan for the nations of the earth. Therefore, it is critical to be walking in His call and to be aligned with His will for your life. *Live Before You Die* is a road map for every believer ready to discover what God has for him and to participate in this great hour of history. In an inspiring yet practical way and with incredible insights and revelation, Daniel Kolenda tackles the questions we all have when seeking our purpose. Communicating in an engaging and motivating style, Kolenda calls believers to give themselves with total abandonment to God's call. This book is not for the fainthearted; it is a radical call of wholehearted consecration. God requires your entire life, but it is in that act of complete surrender that you discover your purpose. Your life was meant to change the course of world history. Anything less is below what God has for you.

—BANNING LIEBSCHER
DIRECTOR, JESUS CULTURE

Live Before You Die will prove to be a great blessing to all who read it. In over fifty years of ministry I have discovered that the question I am asked the most relates to the will of God in an individual's life. Daniel Kolenda has put into one book all that genuine seekers need to know concerning God's will for their lives. His inspired writing explains this in unique simplicity and spells out the way to enter into, enjoy, and do God's will. I unreservedly recommend this book to the body of Christ, young and old. Be prepared for a life-changing read.

—DR. TONY STONE
INTERNATIONAL EVANGELIST AND TEACHER

Daniel Kolenda understands how to live and walk in the will of God! He was in the center of God's will as a student in our ministry school thirteen years ago, and he is in the center of

God's will today as he leads millions of people to Jesus around the world. The practical wisdom in this book will help you discover God's awesome will for your own life and will enable you to walk it out with passion. Who knows what the Lord has planned for you?

—Dr. Michael L. Brown
President of FIRE School of Ministry
Concord, NC

Daniel Kolenda, as many authors, has crafted an expression much like an artist. This work is not a pencil sketch that is abstract and without definition. His new book reminds me of a work on a canvas where every stroke of his pen creates a new burst of color that expresses his soul. Every chapter further releases what he feels he wants us to know about the call of God and His will for our lives.

As a graduate of Brownsville Revival School of Ministry Daniel Kolenda has been on my radar for a while. I believe he is emerging as a voice that will help define evangelism in the twenty-first century.

—Pastor John Kilpatrick
Founder and President, John Kilpatrick Ministries
Daphne, AL

Daniel Kolenda has a fervent passion to preach the gospel of Jesus Christ and a true call to evangelism. His life and ministry reflect the powerful dynamic of a man who yields to the voice of the Holy Spirit. I have known Daniel Kolenda for a number of years and have witnessed firsthand how he has abandoned himself to go into all the world and preach the gospel, calling multitudes to the saving grace of Jesus Christ.

In this powerful and yet conversational writing Daniel Kolenda reveals the heart of God toward those who will hear and obey the voice of the Holy Spirit. With great insight and an expressive authority, this book will lead you to the place of understanding the eternal purpose of answering the call of God upon your life and ministry.

—Evangelist Nathan Morris
Founder and President, Shake the Nations Ministry
Rotherham, UK

I can't think of a more relevant topic than the will of God! So many people spend their entire lives with the constant insecurity of not knowing God's will for them. As a young man who has obviously done well at discovering God's plan for his life, Daniel Kolenda is the right person to write on the topic. Without a doubt, this book will bring clarity into your confusion and help you confirm the purpose on your life. I love this man, his ministry, and this book!

—Pastor Jonathan Stockstill
Bethany World Prayer Center
Baton Rouge, LA

It thrills my soul to see a new generation of holy, humble, and anointed men and women of God emerging on the scene. Daniel Kolenda carries within his heart a zeal and passion for Jesus, as well as an unction to deliver the gospel message with fire. I have met many people in my life who claim the title of "evangelist," but seldom have I crossed paths with those who truly understand the weight of that calling the way this young man does.

Daniel Kolenda's book *Live Before You Die* is a clarion call and a practical road map for all who long to step out of the meaninglessness of living for today and instead make their lives count for eternity. Get ready for God to speak to you. And get ready for action!

—Evangelist Steve Hill
Founder and President, Steve Hill Ministries
Irving, TX

I've used many resources in preparing to preach on "finding God's will," but this is by far the most comprehensive and practical book I've ever encountered. Daniel Kolenda goes deep into this vital subject yet makes it understandable to the reader. It's packed full of vivid illustrations from the Scriptures and personal experience. The only problem was how hard it was to speed-read this book; I found myself stopping often to reflect on one fresh insight or challenge after another.

—Pastor Wayne Hilsden
King of Kings Community Jerusalem

[Wake up to God's will for your life]

LIVE before you die

DANIEL KOLENDA
President of Christ for all Nations

PASSIO

Most CHARISMA HOUSE BOOK GROUP products are available at special quantity discounts for bulk purchase for sales promotions, premiums, fund-raising, and educational needs. For details, write Charisma House Book Group, 600 Rinehart Road, Lake Mary, Florida 32746, or telephone (407) 333-0600.

LIVE BEFORE YOU DIE by Daniel Kolenda
Published by Passio
Charisma Media/Charisma House Book Group
600 Rinehart Road
Lake Mary, Florida 32746
www.charismahouse.com

Unless otherwise noted, all Scripture quotations are from the King James Version of the Bible.

Scripture quotations marked AMP are from the Amplified Bible. Old Testament copyright © 1965, 1987 by the Zondervan Corporation. The Amplified New Testament copyright © 1954, 1958, 1987 by the Lockman Foundation. Used by permission.

Scripture quotations marked ESV are from the Holy Bible, English Standard Version. Copyright © 2001 by Crossway Bibles, a division of Good News Publishers. Used by permission.

Scripture quotations marked NAS are from the New American Standard Bible. Copyright © 1960, 1962, 1963, 1968, 1971, 1972, 1973, 1975, 1977, 1995 by the Lockman Foundation. Used by permission. (www.Lockman.org)

Scripture quotations marked NIV are from the Holy Bible, New International Version. Copyright © 1973, 1978, 1984, International Bible Society. Used by permission.

Scripture quotations marked NKJV are from the New King James Version of the Bible. Copyright © 1979, 1980, 1982 by Thomas Nelson, Inc., publishers. Used by permission.

Scripture quotations marked THE MESSAGE are from *The Message: The Bible in Contemporary English*, copyright © 1993, 1994, 1995, 1996, 2000, 2001, 2002. Used by permission of NavPress Publishing Group.

Cover design by Bill Johnson

Visit the author's website at www.cfan.org.

Library of Congress Control Number: 2012907539
International Standard Book Number: 978-1-61638-716-7
E-book ISBN: 978-1-62136-036-0

While the author has made every effort to provide accurate telephone numbers and Internet addresses at the time of publication, neither the publisher nor the author assumes any responsibility for errors or for changes that occur after publication.

First edition

13 14 15 16 17 — 9 8 7 6 5 4 3 2 1
Printed in the United States of America

DEDICATION

To my four amazing children, in whom I am well pleased:
Elijah, Gloria, London, and Lydia.

Someone asked me who my target audience is for this book. The truth is, I wrote it for you. You were always in my mind as I agonized over every chapter. I prayed that God would help me put into writing what He would want me to say to each of you as you embark on your lifelong journeys of discovering and fulfilling God's will. I can't wait to see what He has in store for you. Always remember, "To whom much is given, much is required."

CONTENTS

Part 4—Five Lingering Questions About God's Will

ACKNOWLEDGMENTS

BOOKS ARE NOT written in a vacuum. Many people helped make this project a reality. My deepest appreciation to:

My beautiful wife, Rebekah. You are the inspiration that moves me, the safe harbor that shelters me, and the anchor that grounds me. Thank you for the sacrifice you make for the work of the gospel. I'm sure your reward in heaven will be greater than mine. I love you, sweetheart!

My four amazing children: Elijah, Gloria, London, and Lydia. I can see God's hand on each of your precious lives. I wrote this book largely as an epistle to you, and many of its lessons I've learned from you. I treasure you more than life itself!

My parents, who invested in me and influenced me more than anyone. Your words and wisdom are ever with me. Thank you for the impeccable example you set of integrity, sincerity, and whole-hearted devotion to Christ.

My four sisters: Sarah, Stephanie, Kimberly, and Michelle. I've shared life with you as with no one else and learned so much from you. You are so precious to me. I could dedicate a book to each of you.

My mentor, friend, and spiritual father, Evangelist Reinhard Bonnke. You have imparted your very life to me. I owe you a debt of gratitude I could never repay. This book is filled with lessons I've learned from you. I love you and Anni dearly. Thank you!

My heroes Peter and Evangeline van den Berg. What you have done for CfaN and for me is beyond description. Your self-sacrifice and humility are without equal. Thank you for the profound impact you've had on my life.

My best friend, Russell Benson. Since the day we met as teenagers at Burger King, we've been as inseparable as David and Jonathan. You have been so instrumental in helping me to discover God's will for my life. Thank you for your faithful friendship.

The CfaN team worldwide. I love you as my own family. We are united by a common, all-consuming passion for the harvest. We will continue to "plunder hell and populate heaven for Calvary's sake."

The entire Charisma Media staff. You have been such a pleasure to work with. Thank you for your excellent spirit.

John Shiver for your invaluable assistance with this book. Our partnership is by divine design.

My Lord and Savior Jesus Christ. Words are not enough, so I give You my whole life just to say, "I love You."

A NOTE TO THE READER

In several places throughout this book you will find QR codes.

These are mobile bar codes embedded with content that smartphone users can access. Each code will instantly direct you to videos and bonus teaching that will further explore the concepts we will be discussing in *Live Before You Die.*

Scan QR code

or visit

LiveBeforeYouDieBook.com

Even if you are not already QR code-savvy, accessing this information will be easy. If you have a smartphone, you can download the QR code reader of your choice (there are many free ones available) and simply scan the codes to access the additional material. If you do not have a smartphone, don't worry. Each QR code has a web address listed below it that will take you to the same special bonus material. Or you can visit LiveBeforeYouDieBook.com and click on the various links.

FOREWORD

Prove what is that good, and acceptable, and perfect, will of God.
—ROMANS 12:2

THE DOCTRINE OF Communism was called the Diamat. Karl
Marx and Friedrich Engels, the founders of socialism, taught
that history was an endless process directed by human conflicts.
One event gave birth to its opposite, they struggled against each
other, then the two came together as one, and the process repeated
itself. They believed the perfect state would eventually emerge. It
would need no laws, and perfection would be achieved. If we did
not accept the communistic way, we were dismissed as reactionaries
and would be left behind by its inevitable developments. Diamat,
however, was contrary to what we saw in real life.

The Christian also believes history is a process but not by virtue
of Diamat. *History advances by the will of God.* Everything remains
under His ultimate authority—even the rebellious. Though people
unquestionably violate God's will within certain limits, the overall
purpose of history progresses "after the counsel of *his* own will"
(Eph. 1:11, emphasis added). Nobody can opt out. This is God's universe, and history is "His story." They operate as He made them to
operate.

Still God made man in His own image, which means we do have the power of choice, decision, and direction. Our will is independent, free, "sovereign." It is this power of will that separates us from the animals and makes us human beings.

God's purpose was that men and women would choose to walk with Him—not just physically but also morally. God designed us to reflect His wonderful nature, and the Bible states that "God is love" (1 John 4:8). He is totally unselfish, forever pouring Himself out like the sun, always giving light and warmth. If man had conformed to that image, he would have created harmony in the universe, for Adam was lord of God's creation.

God made Adam in His own image with the potential of becoming Godlike in character *by choice*, not by force. God did not want to coerce people to love, shape them so they were unable to hate, or shield them mechanically from being selfish. He wanted man to exercise his free will and choose His way.

God intended humans to use their free will as a gift to rule the earth on His behalf. But if used wrongly, that free will could become dangerous. Sadly Adam became victim to his own power of choice: he chose contrary to God's will. The will of God and the will of man clashed, creating a fallen and unjust world. This is the essence of what we call sin. It is the tension between the Creator and His creatures. Now we live within that conflict between God's will and man's.

People have often posed this conundrum: If God's will is supreme, how can we be free? If God knows all that will be, how can the future be changed by our free will? The answer for some is that we actually have no free will. Still others go as far as to say that nothing is free—whatever happens, God chooses and wills. This is called fatalism. In that philosophy you are safe until a bullet comes with your number on it. The Muslims call this *kismet*, that everything happens according to the will of Allah. Each destiny is fixed. The Greeks likewise talked about the Fates weaving the future. Other early thinkers said that everything was set and would keep on repeating forever. In these ways people wrestled with how "God's will" could coexist with mankind's "free will."

But the biblical solution is rather simple. God Himself gave man free will, and the way He operates His will alongside man's freedom is no problem to Him. It is only a problem to us because we cannot see all of time and eternity at once as He can. God is perfect and full of joy, and His will is behind creation as He works out His purposes. He is moving sinful history toward His sinless perfection and happiness in Christ. God's will is to bring all of creation back into glorious harmony with His Son, Jesus!

Jesus will reign as King of kings. That means His counsel will prevail—His mercy, goodness, and love will regulate and permeate everything on the earth. Kings will look after the everyday affairs, but the King of kings will rule the kings and ensure that no legislation will lack His wisdom and righteousness. We look forward to that day when God's will is done perfectly "in earth, as it is in heaven" (Matt. 6:10).

In the meantime the will of God is not being done perfectly throughout the earth. Even Jesus declared that He would have saved Jerusalem, but the people would not let Him (Matt. 23:37). This is why He taught us to pray that His will would be done on the earth.

We know what His will is because He has revealed it to us. God does not keep it a secret. He has revealed His will to us in His Word. Even though on the one hand God's awesome ways are past finding out, He has come into our world and opened Himself up to inspection and investigation. He entered relationship with us through His Son and shows us His plans in His Word. As Paul said, "In all wisdom and insight He made known to us the mystery of His will" (Eph. 1:8–9, NAS). The true God does not desire for His will to remain a mystery to us.

But God allows us freedom of choice. Some talk about how God has a plan and detailed blueprint for every life. I don't know where that idea comes from, but it is widespread—almost like an epidemic. Such thinking has caused too many Christians to sit and do nothing, waiting for God to "reveal" His specific plan to them. Yes, He guides us, but *only as we are moving.* He directs *our* paths not His paths! He respects our will. I do not understand people who suppose it is very difficult to know God's will for their lives. Is God like that? If you called a plumber to do some work for you, and he came to your house to do his work, would you not tell him what job needs done? Or would you remain silent and keep him guessing every day he came by?

Some wonder why God doesn't answer their prayers and show them His exact will for them. They do not realize that they may already be doing what God wants. They assume He must have something else for them to do, something grander or more exciting. Yet what He really wants is for us to be like Him—to love like Him and serve like Him—wherever we are.

God has shown us His will. Now He wants us to emerge and do it by working for Him and with Him. He offers us the same delight and pleasure in all good works that He enjoys. For God's will is good. It is always "goodwill," always concerned with people's eternal well-being, and always producing good fruit in the lives we touch.

Daniel Kolenda has laid out the truth of God's will very well indeed. He is one of those young men Joel said would "prophesy" (Joel 2:28). He carries a powerful anointing of gospel power and gospel knowledge. This book is an example of that. It is a "prophecy" for this generation, calling them—calling you!—to rise and do the will of Him who rules time and eternity. I highly recommend Daniel Kolenda to you. Read this book more than once. It will bless you greatly, and God will use it to "equip you in every good thing to do His will" (Heb. 13:21, NAS).

—REINHARD BONNKE

Reinhard Bonnke is founder of the international ministry Christ for all Nations, where Daniel Kolenda serves as president. Since the early 1980s Bonnke has conducted citywide meetings across Africa with as many as 1.6 million people in attendance in a single meeting. At the time of this writing the ministry had documented 68 million decisions for Christ since they started recording registered decision cards in 1987.

Scan QR code

or visit
LiveBeforeYouDieBook.com/intro

INTRODUCTION

THOUSANDS HAD GATHERED to witness the brief spectacle that would unfold between the white sand and blue sky, the largest theater on earth. We waited for what seemed like ages with our eyes trained on the horizon. No one wanted to miss the big moment. And then it happened. What an amazing sight! Even from quite a distance the eruption of energy was awe-inspiring. The solid rocket boosters ignited, producing an explosion that generated 2.9 million pounds of thrust at liftoff![1] The ground began to tremble as the spacecraft raced skyward, leaving a thick trail of smoke behind. Within seconds it had broken the bonds of gravity and was out of sight. I stood on that beach in Titusville, Florida, with my wife and kids in amazement as we watched, up close, history in the making: the final launch of the space shuttle *Atlantis*.

After the shuttle penetrated the mesosphere at an altitude of about thirty-one miles,[2] the rocket boosters that had expended themselves were no longer needed and were ejected to return to earth. As *Atlantis* was racing to space for the final time, I saw in those powerful boosters an equally splendid metaphor. The rockets, though powerful, do not exist for themselves. They are designed to propel something forward that is greater than they are. Their glory is in exhausting themselves for a superior purpose. Long after they have fallen away, the shuttle will keep moving forward. It is the shuttle and its mission that give meaning to the rocket's existence.

Your Life as a Headline

June 25, 2009, is one of those days I will never forget. Two of my generation's most famous icons died the same day, within hours of each other. Farrah Fawcett was the beautiful actress from the TV show *Charlie's Angels,* and Michael Jackson was the undisputed "King of Pop." Both succumbed to untimely deaths that shocked the world and kept every news outlet buzzing for weeks. I must have watched the same footage for hours that day, hoping to be distracted from the overwhelming sense of temporal impermanence that made me a bit more thoughtful and sentimental than usual.

The lives of Farrah Fawcett and Michael Jackson were so huge, so important, so publicized, yet the things they were best known for were so meaningless in light of eternity. So Michael Jackson had the best-selling album of all time. So Farrah Fawcett was beautiful and won a People's Choice Award. What eternal difference does it make? If you stand back and read their obituaries in the larger context of the world and of what matters, there is an overwhelming sense of utter meaninglessness, and yet, in the world's terms, they were two of the most illustrious figures among us.

Most of us will never make the evening news with our passing, but just imagine for a minute that you did. Imagine that CNN, NBC, ABC, CBS, and Fox News were all running marathon coverage of your death and talking about the significance of your life. Imagine that they had to put your entire earthly existence into a one-sentence news crawl or a front-page headline. What would it say? Better yet, what would you want it to say? What one purpose would make your entire life worthwhile to you?

If you listen to the feel-good wisdom of the age calling out to you from television and music, magazines and self-help books, you may come to believe that the chief end of being is finding happiness and success in this world. "The sky is the limit," they will tell you. "You can reach the stars and become one yourself." "You can be anything you want to be." "You are the master of your destiny."

But the reality is, how much money you make, whom you know, and the notoriety you receive are very insignificant in and of themselves. One day all the material possessions you have accumulated and fought to obtain will be divided among relatives or sold for pennies at a garage sale. If you're like most people, your name will one day be unknown, and your face will be unrecognizable. Like the rocket boosters on the space shuttle I described earlier, your mortal life force will one day fall away and disappear into an ocean of obscurity. But, my friend, that is not the end of the story. Although our lives will one day come to an end, the kingdom of God will keep moving forward to victory, and herein lies our greatest opportunity. With our mortal hands we can help to build God's eternal kingdom—and that is the greatest privilege any human being could have!

> The purpose of your existence is not to achieve your own happiness or success. Your role is to advance a cause greater than yourself.

This book is not about reaching your dreams or becoming a star, because in the end none of those things matter at all. Before the contents of this book will have any meaning or value in your life, you must understand that the purpose of your existence is not to achieve your own happiness or success. You are not the space shuttle in my metaphor; you are the rocket booster. Your role is to advance a cause greater than yourself. The ripples your life produces will continue to impact the world for better or worse far beyond your earthly existence, but your life will be only as meaningful as what it propels forward.

Lose Your Life—and Find It!

On the wall of the south choir aisle of Westminster Abbey hangs a memorial stone to John and Charles Wesley that says, "God buries His workmen, but carries on His work." The Wesley brothers' lives were like rocket boosters in the hands of God. The Wesleys have been dead for many generations, but God's eternal kingdom is still moving forward, and the small part they played in this divine initiative makes their lives valuable and significant.

Before he died, Paul told Timothy, "I am already being poured out as a drink offering, and the time of my departure is at hand" (2 Tim. 4:6, NKJV). Paul saw his life as expendable for the sake of the gospel. He would be poured out like a drink offering and then drop off like exhausted rocket boosters, but not without having done something of eternal importance. With his mortal and finite life he helped to propel God's ever-lasting kingdom forward. That knowledge brought Paul complete satisfaction.

> If you really want your life to count, you have to throw it away into the service of the One who gave you life in the first place.

The reality is that everyone is expending his life and burning through the finite fuel he's been given, yet so many give very little thought to what they are living for. Let me ask you, my friend, what are you living for? What will make your life count? What are you propelling forward with your time, energy, finances, and passion?

Jesus said, "For whosoever will save his life shall lose it; but whosoever shall lose his life for my sake and the gospel's, the same shall save it" (Mark 8:35). If you really, really want your life to count, there is only one way to make that happen: you have to throw it away. You have to throw your life away into the service of the One who gave you life in the first place.

Saved to Serve

"If I were to save your life, what would you do?" This was the question Cyrus, the king of Persia, asked a rebel chieftain named Cagular, whom he had captured and was about to execute. Cagular replied, "King, I would serve you the rest of my days." We would tend to see Cagular's pledge of allegiance to Cyrus as nothing more than a reasonable offer in exchange for the king's merciful pardon. Cagular also recognized that if the king were to save his life, he would be indebted to the king and therefore obliged to serve him.

In Romans 1:14–15 Paul said, "I am debtor both to the Greeks, and to the Barbarians; both to the wise, and to the unwise. So, as much as in me is, I am ready to preach the gospel to you that are at Rome also." You see, the traditional thinking among the religious elite in Paul's day was that, as God's chosen people, any ministry offered the Gentiles was a magnanimous handout to undeserving heathen. But Paul saw himself as one who had been shown great mercy by God, and that made him a debtor to the rest of mankind. For him to preach the gospel to the Gentiles was not a charitable condescension; it was the only appropriate response he could have to God's amazing grace and mercy. Paul realized he had been saved to serve.

Paul went on to tell the Romans that they should also present themselves to God as a living sacrifice, and then he added, "which is your reasonable service" (Rom. 12:1). In other words this is not some generous favor you are doing for God. He purchased you and redeemed you with the blood of His Son. He set you free from sin and bondage. He has blessed you with every spiritual blessing in heavenly places in Christ. In light of all He has done for you, your reciprocate service to Him is only "reasonable." You have been saved to serve.

you have been saved to serve!

5

Compelled by Love

"Oh that one would give me drink of the water of the well of Bethlehem, which is by the gate!" sighed King David (2 Sam. 23:15). When three soldiers overheard his wishful musing, they reached for their swords and disappeared into the night. They had not been commanded to act and were under no obligation to do so, but they were driven by a force more compelling than any call of duty: love for their king. That is what compelled them to break through the camp of the Philistines, draw out the water, and bring it to David.

David was so touched by this exploit that he could not bring himself to drink the water. Instead he poured it out before the Lord. It wasn't the risk they had taken that impressed him. Soldiers were required to risk their lives as a matter of course, but this was different. They did not do this for Israel, for Judah, for the war, or even for the battle. This was a personal offering for David and certainly the most costly gift this king had ever been given.

Someone once told me, "I don't have a burden for any particular nation." In his mind this disqualified (or excused) him from ministry. But at the end of the day if the burden we feel for people is our sole motivation for preaching the gospel or serving the Lord, it is just another form of humanism.

After Jesus had risen from the dead, He found that Peter had gone back to his old occupation—fishing. After cooking breakfast for Peter, Jesus pointed to one of the fish and asked this question, "'Simon [Peter] son of John, do you truly love me more than these?' 'Yes, Lord,' he said, 'you know that I love you.' Jesus said, 'Feed my lambs'" (John 21:15, NIV). Notice that Jesus didn't say, "Peter, do you love My lambs?" Then, "Feed My lambs." Rather Jesus asked, "Peter, do you love *Me*?" Peter's ministry to the sheep was to be motivated primarily by his love for Christ, not his love for the lambs.

Do you love Jesus? That is the real question. And that should be enough to drive us to pour out our lives in service before our King. This is the ambition that reigns supreme over all others, including the desire to advance the kingdom of God, edify the people of God, or even to reach the lost and dying world. The first and finest motivation anyone can have is just love—love for the One who loved us so much He poured out His tears, blood, and life.

When we receive His gift of life, which cost Jesus His life, how can we spend it in the pursuit of our own ambitions, lusts, and gratification? God forbid. Instead, in reverent awe and profound love, we are compelled to pour our lives back out before Him like a drink offering, holding nothing back, giving everything we are in the service of the only King who will reign forever and ever. Make no mistake—this is not a waste. It is our reasonable service. We have been saved to serve.

Is What You're Living for Worth Christ Dying for?

An American soldier in the Vietnam War was about to step on an anti-personnel land mine that was hidden from his sight. His comrade across the battlefield, who could see the impending disaster from his vantage point, stood up from behind his protective barricade and shouted a life-saving warning to his friend. At that moment the brave young man received a gunshot wound that ended his life. A couple of years later, at an honorary memorial service in the United States, the soldier whose life had been saved from the land mine had a chance to meet the wife and son of his deceased friend. The son, who was only seven years old, had never gotten a chance to really know his father. The soldier could tell that this boy's heart was broken, so he knelt down next to him and put his hand on the child's shoulder. "I want you to know," the soldier said, "your father saved my life." The little boy looked up at him with tears streaming down his cheeks. "Sir," he said, "were you worth it?"

Leonard Ravenhill once asked the question, "Is what you're living for worth Christ dying for?" We were not saved so that we could be polished, decorative knickknacks sitting on God's shelf filling space in heaven for eternity. We have been saved for a purpose, and the fulfillment of that purpose is the only acceptable reaction we can have to the great gift of salvation we have received. You have an obligation, a debt, a compulsion, and a liability to the One who laid down His life for you. You have been saved, not for salvation's sake, but you have been saved to serve.

In light of these things what then should we do? Perhaps you feel a desire to respond by offering your life as a "rocket booster" to propel God's kingdom forward, but you are not sure where to begin. When Saul, who later became the apostle Paul, met the Lord on the road to Damascus, this was his question: "Lord, what do You want me to do?" (Acts 9:6, NKJV). And this is where our journey begins, with a simple question. The question is not, "What do I want to do with my life?" but, "Lord, what do *You* want me to do with my life?"

This book is different from many similar books in that it is not primarily about career choices, personal fulfillment, or self-actualization. Whether this journey takes you to the mission field or medical school, whether you become a construction worker, businessman, chef, or pastor, discovering God's will for your life is not a matter of determining what *you* want but what *He* wants. It is a spiritual quest of utmost significance, and the Holy Spirit must lead it. For that reason I invite you to begin this journey by praying the following prayer for guidance and direction:

> *Heavenly Father, I present myself to You today as a living sacrifice. Because You gave Your Son for me, I give myself to You fully. This is my reasonable service. I lay my dreams and desires at Your feet and ask that Your will would be done in my life. Use my mortal hands to build Your eternal kingdom. Use my life to propel Your purposes forward. In Jesus's name, amen.*

PART 1

FIVE BASIC QUESTIONS ABOUT GOD'S WILL

Chapter 1

DOES GOD REALLY HAVE A
PLAN FOR MY LIFE?

IT WAS HARVEST time in Israel, and a palpable sense of anxiety was in the air. At any moment the wary farmers might lift their eyes to see a tidal wave of Midianite soldiers pouring down from the hills like a flash flood from a broken dam. The Bible describes the Midianites as a nation of "grasshoppers" (Judg. 7:12). Whenever the harvest was ripe, they would descend upon Israel's fields and crops in vast numbers like a swarm of locusts, leaving nothing in their wake but destruction and desolation. The Israelites went on the defensive, hunkering down in caves, hiding in the mountains, and building protective strongholds. The nervous harvesters quickly reaped what they could and hid it away in anticipation of an imminent invasion.

God had a plan to deliver Israel from the hand of Midian, and He had chosen just the man for the job, but God's choice seemed highly unlikely. Gideon was not a superhero by any stretch of the imagination. He was a victim of his society's ills, a man who had been influenced by the climate of cowardice that had crippled and enslaved the Israelites. He was such a prisoner of fear that he would hide in a winepress to thresh his small harvest of wheat (Judg. 6:11).

A winepress is no place to thresh wheat; it's like washing your clothes in the dishwasher. But Gideon had chosen this inappropriate place because he was afraid of the Midianites. He was afraid of losing his harvest and his life, so he hid both underground. It was in this dungeon of fear that the Lord found Gideon, frustrated, trembling, and perspiring.

> And the Angel of the Lord appeared to him and said to him, The Lord is with you, you mighty man of [fearless] courage.
> —JUDGES 6:12, AMP

No one would have anticipated the Lord's declaration that day. "Gideon," the Lord says, "you are a mighty man of fearless courage!" Where others saw a coward, God saw a deliverer!

I'm so glad God doesn't see us the way we so often see ourselves. When we look in the mirror, we might see someone who is under-educated or inexperienced. We might see someone who belongs to the wrong social class, race, or gender. We might see someone who is too young or too old. And there are always a million excuses why God can't use us. But God sees more in us than we see in ourselves, and our obstacles, failures, and shortcomings do not intimidate Him.

I am also glad that God doesn't see us the way other people do. Many times when we begin to break out of the old patterns and mind-sets that have held us back, rejecting the status quo and looking for higher ground, our greatest opponents are close friends, fellow church members, and even our own relatives. In fact, it's interesting to note that the Midianites, being descendants of Abraham, were actually cousins of the Israelites. It was these "family members," if you will, who had so oppressed Israel that they were cowering in fear rather than living victoriously. The enemy knows how to use those closest to us to bring discouragement. They say, "Who do you think you are? Do you think you're better than us? We've known you since you were a child. We've seen all your failures, and we know your faults. You are just one of us. Get back in your place!"

Some time ago I became interested in purchasing an aquarium. As I began to research this project, I was amazed to discover all the different types of aquariums that can be bought. There are large ones and small ones, freshwater and saltwater. There are aquariums for fish, aquariums for corals, aquariums for reptiles, and aquariums for invertebrates. What really fascinated me was the aquarium for crabs. I discovered that these particular aquariums had no lids, and I was amused when I learned why. Apparently when you have an aquarium for crabs, you don't need a cover because if one crab tries to climb out, the others will reach up and pull him back down again. I thought to myself, "I know a lot of crabby Christians." We don't like to see someone succeed where we have failed. Envy and jealousy often make God's children competitors and rivals. Often hurtful and judgmental words have wounded brothers and sisters, dragged them down, and kept them from realizing their potential.

Sadly this happens all the time in the church world. Just as God is elevating one pastor and blessing his ministry, the other pastors in town oppose him with slander and gossip. They will do everything they can to pull him back down into the aquarium of church as usual. Such a pastor, church, or Christian should take comfort. Someone once told me, "Pity you get for free, but jealousy must be earned." Jesus Himself was delivered up by His own people to be crucified—because they envied Him (Matt. 27:18). How often have we been discouraged because of what someone else thought or said about us? Fortunately the wonderful reality is that God doesn't see us the way other people do.

God—the Master Artist

In the winepress we find a trembling, perspiring coward hiding for his life when the Angel of the Lord appears to Gideon and calls him a "mighty man of [fearless] courage." At first those words almost sound like cruel sarcasm, but there was no smirk on the angel's face. God was not mocking Gideon, nor did He have Gideon confused with someone else. God saw something in Gideon that no one else saw, including Gideon himself. How comforting it is to know that God's ways are not our ways and His thoughts are not our thoughts. Oh, my friend, when you understand what God sees when He looks at you, it will change your life. Let me explain it this way.

David Sculpture
Scan QR code

or visit
LiveBeforeYouDieBook.com/1

In the early 1500s a twenty-five-year-old artist and sculptor labored tirelessly with hammer and chisel over a colossal block of cold marble. Other artists had rejected the stone because it had defects, so it sat untouched for several decades before this young sculptor saw something beautiful in it. He worked night and day with obsessive dedication. When someone asked him why he was working so hard on that old stone, he replied, "Because there is an angel in that rock that wants to come out."[1] Nearly three years after starting his work, the young artist, Michelangelo, unveiled his enduring masterpiece: a seventeen-foot-tall sculpture that today is known the world over as *David*.

Anyone who is an artisan will acknowledge that before a masterpiece is ever crafted, it exists in the mind of its creator. Before a brush strokes the canvas, before a chisel touches the stone, before the clay is placed on the potter's wheel, before the artist creates a painting, sculpture, or piece of pottery, before the artist has anything tangible to display, he first and foremost has a dream. In the artist's mind he already sees what he will create before it exists in the physical world. Michelangelo saw something in that block of stone long before anyone else did. Other artists saw impossible defects and imperfections, but Michelangelo saw a masterpiece trapped in that rejected rock, and he worked diligently to set it free.

Our God is the master artist! Consider the unfathomable wonder of creation, which even in its fallen condition gives us a fleeting glimpse into the genius of its Creator who, in His eternal mind, saw every detail down to the smallest particle while there was still nothing. Just think about this: the architect of the universe spoke the worlds into existence, but He crafted Adam with His own hands and breathed into him with His own mouth! God has crowned His creation with a masterpiece, which is distinguished because it is "handmade" by the great Creator! And God continues to fashion mankind with His own hands. Psalm 139:13 says, "For You formed my inward parts; You wove me in my mother's womb" (NAS).

> Whatever God's dream for your life might be, one thing is for sure: His will for your life is beyond what you could ask or think!

The Master of the universe, the eternal, immortal, invisible, all-wise God, made you with His own hands! But before He began to weave you together in your mother's womb, He saw you in His eternal mind, down to the smallest detail. And before you were ever born, He had a dream for your life. Perhaps as He was weaving you together in your mother's womb, He said, "I'm going to make this boy into a mighty man of fearless courage!" Or, "I'm going to make this little girl into a mighty prophetess to her generation!" Whatever His dream for your life might be, one thing is for sure: His will for your life is beyond what you could ask or think!

Obvious Evidence of Purpose

In thousands of classrooms all over the world teachers are indoctrinating naïve and impressionable students with the notion that they are an accident, the result of millions of years of random anomalies and lucky deformities, or that what they do with their lives is just a matter of preference and there is no divine designer who created them. But the Bible tells us that God designed us with a purpose in mind. Psalm 139:14 says we have been "fearfully and wonderfully made." It is only in recent years, with advances in science, that we are beginning to understand just how true those words are. Your body is a mind-blowing feat of engineering—an unbelievably complex design. Did you know that your body employs the aid of more than two hundred muscles just to take a single step?[2]

Consider the human eye, the design of which is so elegant and complex scientists still don't fully understand how it works. It moves on average one hundred thousand separate times in a single day; conducts its own maintenance work while we sleep; has automatic aim, focus, and aperture adjustment; provides color, stereoscopic 3-D images; and can function from almost total darkness to bright light automatically.[3] It can discern more than sixteen million color hues,[4] including seven hundred shades of gray.[5] In fact, Charles Darwin himself said, "To suppose that the eye with all its inimitable contrivances for adjusting the focus to different distances, for admitting different amounts of light, and for the correction of spherical and chromatic aberration, could have been formed by natural selection, seems, I freely confess, absurd in the highest degree."[6]

Your skin can contain in *one square centimeter*: 3,000 sensory cells, 12 heat sensors, 200 pain sensors, 700 sweat glands, 1 yard of blood vessels, 3 million cells, and 4 yards of nerves[7] that send messages to our brains at speeds of up to 200 miles per hour.[8] Your brain weighs only about 3 pounds yet contains 12 billion cells, each of which is connected to 10,000 other brain cells, making 120 trillion connections.[9] It generates more electrical impulses in a single day than all of the world's telephones put together[10] yet uses less energy than a refrigerator light.[11]

The DNA molecules in your body contain the most densely packed and elaborately detailed assembly of information in the known universe.[12] Their code is so unbelievably complex that if you printed out all of your body's DNA chemical "letters" in books, it is estimated that it would create enough books to fill the Grand Canyon fifty times![13]

Of course, I could go on and on and on citing the wonders of gravity and magnetism that science still cannot fully explain, the flawless rhythm of the solar system, the perfect balance of nitrogen and oxygen in earth's atmosphere that makes life possible, the amazing order in nature that forms a self-supporting system of life, reproduction, and waste disposal. But is any of this necessary? What more evidence do we need that our world has been created with intelligence and purpose than the beauty, order, and design we see around us and within us?

No person who has ever been created is an accident, a fluke of nature, the hapless by-product of the union of a man and a woman, or the result of millions of years of unguided mishaps. Every person who has ever been born is a unique creation, an intentional work of art crafted by the hand of the master artist.

> Our God is the master artist! He sees "an angel" in the rock of your life, and He wants to set it free.

God told Jeremiah, "Before I formed you in the womb, I knew you; before you were born I sanctified you; I ordained you a prophet to the nations" (Jer. 1:5, NKJV). God both knew and crafted a destiny for Jeremiah the prophet even before his birth. John the Baptist was filled with the Holy Spirit and called to be the forerunner of Jesus even before he was born (Luke 1:15). Samson was called to be a great deliverer before he was conceived in his mother's womb (Judg. 13:4–5).

Isaiah 46:10 says God declares "the end from the beginning, and from ancient times things that are not yet done" (NKJV). Romans

4:17 says that God "quickeneth the dead, and calleth those things which be not as though they were." Psalm 139:15–16 says, "You know me inside and out, you know every bone in my body; you know exactly how I was made, bit by bit, how I was sculpted from nothing into something. Like an open book, you watched me grow from conception to birth; all the stages of my life were spread out before you, the days of my life all prepared before I'd even lived one day" (THE MESSAGE).

God called Jeremiah a "prophet" before he was born. God called John a "forerunner" before he was born. God called Samson a "deliverer" before he was born. And this is why, even though God found a trembling, perspiring coward in the winepress, He called Gideon "a mighty man of fearless courage." God saw inside Gideon the potential He had created in him before he was born. While Gideon was still in his mother's womb, God called him a mighty man of valor, and God never gave up on that dream for Gideon's life.

Someone once told me, "I don't believe in God." I said, "That's unfortunate, because God believes in you." Before you were even born, before God began to fashion and form you, before He began to knit you together in your mother's womb, He had a dream for you and a plan for your life. He had a holy calling for you to fulfill. Paul told Timothy that it was God "who hath saved us, and called us with an holy calling, not according to our works, but according to his own purpose and grace, which was given us in Christ Jesus before the world began" (2 Tim. 1:9).

Gideon was full of imperfections, he was not esteemed highly in the eyes of other people, and he was a downright looser in his own eyes. But God looked at Gideon just as Michelangelo looked at that rejected piece of marble. In Gideon God could see beauty where everyone else saw only defects. My friend, you might have been written off by everyone else. You might think your life is far too flawed to ever be something beautiful. But our God is the master artist! He sees "an angel" in the rock of your life, and He wants to set it free. Throughout your life, no matter where you go or what you do, whenever God looks at you, He sees inside of you the potential He placed within you, and He is always calling to that potential as He called Lazarus out of the grave, "Come out!" God wants to take your life from the junkyard of the devil and turn it into a masterpiece, a trophy of His amazing grace and mercy.

The Goodwill of God

It's amazing to think that even after the Angel of the Lord had appeared to Gideon and told him plainly about God's goodwill toward him, Gideon was slow to believe it.

> And Gideon said to him, O sir, if the Lord is with us, why is all this befallen us? And where are all His wondrous works of which our fathers told us, saying, Did not the Lord bring us up from Egypt? But now the Lord has forsaken us and given us into the hand of Midian. The Lord turned to him and said, Go in this your might, and you shall save Israel from the hand of Midian. Have I not sent you? Gideon said to Him, Oh Lord, how can I deliver Israel? Behold, my clan is the poorest in Manasseh, and I am the least in my father's house.
>
> —Judges 6:13–15, amp

Just as Gideon did, many people struggle with feelings of inferiority. They may have been abused or rejected and as a result have low self-esteem and little self-worth. They may say to themselves, "But I did not come from a wealthy family." "I do not have a good education." "I'm not smart enough." "I was abused." "I do not have any talents or abilities." "I could never succeed."

When Gideon looked in the mirror, all he could see were disadvantages and shortcomings. He doubted that he was capable of greatness and was not convinced the Lord had picked the right man for the job. But the Lord knew exactly what Gideon needed to hear, and He spoke words that went right to the heart of Gideon's inadequacy: "The Lord said to him, Surely I will be with you" (Judg. 6:16, AMP).

These must be the most comforting words in the entire world. To know that God is with you and that He is for you—this is the ultimate assurance. These were the words Gideon needed to hear, and these are also the words you need to hear deep within your spirit as you begin this journey of discovering God's will for your life. Jesus knew you would need to hear them, and this is why He said, "I will never leave you nor forsake you" (Heb. 13:5, NKJV) and again in Matthew 28:20, "Lo, I am with you always, even to the end of the age" (NKJV).

Romans 8:31–32 says, "What then shall we say to these things? If God is for us, who can be against us? He who did not spare His own Son, but delivered Him up for us all, how shall He not with Him also freely give us all things?" (NKJV). God is *for* you and *not* against you! Do you need evidence? In this passage of Scripture Paul points to the cross as the ultimate proof of God's goodwill toward us. If God was willing to give His own Son for us, how much more can we trust that He will gladly and generously give us anything and everything we need?

Do you feel like a failure? Does the past haunt you and define you? Do you have a difficult time believing God is on your side and has your best interests in mind? It's time for you to get a revelation of the goodness of God. He is not looking for perfect people, and He is not intimidated by your past. He desires "to console those who mourn in Zion, to give them beauty for ashes, the oil of joy for mourning, the garment of praise for the spirit of heaviness; that they may be called trees of righteousness, the planting of the LORD, that He may be glorified" (Isa. 61:3, NKJV).

Paul wrote about this same truth in Romans 8:28 when he said, "And we know that *all things* work together for *good* to those who love God, to those who are the called according to *His purpose*"

(NKJV, emphasis added). When we understand this reality and it becomes part of the fabric of who we are, then we will begin to view every circumstance, both positive and negative, as a situation God can put to work for our good and the furtherance of His purposes. Salvation, atonement, forgiveness, justification, regeneration, redemption, reconciliation—these are all words used to describe what God desires to do in our lives. Turning ashes into beauty is not an auxiliary benefit of the Christian experience; it is the heart of the gospel, and it is God's will for you!

Jeremiah 29:11 says, "For I know the thoughts that I think toward you, says the LORD, thoughts of peace and not of evil, to give you a future and a hope" (NKJV). Does God have a plan for your life? The answer is a resounding yes! But it's even better than that. Not only does God have a plan, but He also has a *good* plan that is "exceedingly abundantly above all that we ask or think" (Eph. 3:20, NKJV). And with that confidence, we can begin our journey, "looking unto Jesus, the author and finisher of our faith" (Heb. 12:2, NKJV), knowing that "He who has begun a good work in you will complete it" (Phil. 1:6, NKJV).

Chapter 2

HAVE I MISUNDERSTOOD GOD'S WILL?

ALL FOUR GOSPELS tell of the triumphal entry of Jesus into Jerusalem, and an interesting fact is mentioned. The Bible says the people "took branches of palm trees, and went forth to meet him, and cried, Hosanna: Blessed is the King of Israel that cometh in the name of the Lord" (John 12:13). Have you ever wondered why they waved palm branches and cried, "Hosanna"? The reason is not what many people think.

Political zealots had used the palm branch as a symbol for quite some time. At one point the palm was used on coins minted during an insurrectionary rebellion, and they conjured images of Maccabean resistance. The palm branches seem to be an indication of the nationalistic and political expectations the people had for Jesus. This is further confirmed by the word *hosanna* itself, which means "save, please" in Aramaic. But Jesus was a great disappointment to the people of Israel, and a few days after waving their branches and crying "Hosanna," they turned on Him and cried, "Crucify Him!"[1]

The nation of Israel as a whole rejected their Messiah because He did not fit into their preconceived expectations. They were looking for a political deliverer, a man of war and conquest. They were looking for a king who would overthrow the oppressive Roman government and return the nation to its former glory. Instead they found a man of peace, meek and humble, riding on a lowly donkey rather than a warrior's stallion. To this day Jews around the world are praying for the arrival of their long-awaited Messiah, but He came two thousand years ago, and many still do not recognize Him because He is not what they are looking for.

Preconceptions produce misconceptions that can blind us to what is obvious, and this happens to many people as they seek God's will for their lives. God already has a purpose for you that has been in existence since before you were born! In fact, God may have already revealed His will to you, and you might be looking right at it, but misconceptions might be keeping you from recognizing it. In this chapter I want to unmask three common misconceptions about God's will.

Misconception #1: God's Will Is Hard to Figure Out

A scientist took a group of young researchers on an expedition into the desert to study various types of cacti. But their mission was cut short when their vehicle broke down in the middle of the vast barren wilderness. The scientist who was heading the expedition was very familiar with the territory and was confident they could make it back to civilization. But to his great dismay, after two days of walking it became obvious that they were hopelessly lost. The last canteen yielded its final drop of water, and desperation began to set in as the sunburned and dehydrated group realized they would most likely die in this desert.

Suddenly one of the researchers shouted to the rest of the group, "There, in the distance—it's an oasis!" Cheers and cries of excitement rang out from the haggard team, but the lead scientist bowed his head dejectedly. "I'm sorry to tell you this," he said as he collapsed into the sand, "but what you are seeing is only a mirage." The young researchers simply refused to believe it. They took their canteens and ran toward the shimmering reflection in the distance, hoping upon hope that what they were seeing was real.

After a few minutes they came close enough to see clearly. Sturdy palm trees huddled cozily around a sparkling, spring-fed pool of refreshing water, and they jumped in with both feet. They splashed and drank as their strength returned, and after refilling their canteens, they headed back to take the wonderful report to the lead scientist. But their joy turned to sorrow when they found his body, limp and lifeless, lying in the spot where he had collapsed.

God's will is often like that oasis in the desert; it is a life-giving source of purpose and reason for being. In most cases God's will is not a faraway mystery but something within view and something accessible. Yet what is right in front of our faces is often the easiest thing to dismiss, and God's will may be so obvious that we overlook it thinking that it must be more difficult.

Have you ever noticed that when a person first becomes a believer, he seems to easily hear God's voice and sense His leading? Often the more mature we become and the more we learn, the more complicated and confusing things become. The scientist in my story died because he had already decided that the oasis in the distance was too good to be true. He was educated and experienced. He knew mirages were common phenomena in the desert. But his knowledge and experience prevented him from recognizing what was right in front of him.

Have you heard sermons about God's will that left you feeling discouraged and more confused than ever? Have you been led to believe that you need to be a prophet to know what God is saying? Does it seem as if the more you search, the less you find? Perhaps the most valuable thing you can learn is that you need to unlearn a lot of the things you have learned. Those things that bring confusion and overanalysis need to be dropped. Start with simple, childlike faith. Trust that God has a plan He is trying to reveal to you. Believe that He wants you to discover it more than you want to discover it! Rest in the assurance that He's not trying to trick or puzzle you. Remember that He is not the author of confusion (1 Cor. 14:33), and He does not create mirages to deceive you. Discovering God's will for your life is *not* difficult. Let's simplify!

Misconception #2: God Always Reveals His Will Suddenly and Dramatically

Often when people say God has not revealed His will for their lives, what they really mean is that they have not heard an audible voice from heaven. Of course there are moments when God speaks in very dramatic ways, but more often than not God reveals His will in a much less extravagant fashion, and it often unfolds slowly, layer by layer over time rather than in a single, earth-shattering epiphany.

Consider Abraham, the father of the Israelite nation, whom God called to "get out of your country, from your family, and from your father's house, to a land that I will show you" (Gen. 12:1, NKJV). God asked Abraham to leave everything familiar for something completely unknown. God's call to Abraham did not include specific coordinates, just a call to go. As Abraham obeyed, God revealed His plan one step at a time.

If God revealed His ultimate plan for our lives from the beginning, we would often find ourselves chasing a dream rather than following Him. God didn't want to just *send* Abraham to his inheritance; God wanted to *lead* him there. In following God, Abraham made an amazing discovery. The land and the legacy that God would give him was something wonderful indeed, but there was another reward that would make all others pale in comparison. "Abram," the Lord says, "I am…your exceedingly great reward" (Gen. 15:1, NKJV).

> God's will is never revealed in such a way that it negates our need for dependence upon Him.

If you think you have it all figured out and you know exactly where God is going to take you and how He's going to get you there, be prepared for disappointment. God's will is never revealed in such a way that it negates our need for dependence upon Him. Ultimately whether or not we fulfill God's will for our lives depends on whether or not we follow Him. In the end we will all discover that the *real* prize was not the perfect career, wonderful spouse, or right education. The real reward for following God is God Himself.

The full revelation of God's will rarely comes as a sudden epiphany. He calls to us to see if we will follow even without knowing all the details. When He sees that we take a step of obedience, then He gives us the next step.

Recently in an interview I was asked how God had shown me that it was His will for me to be doing what I am doing in ministry. I think the interviewer was hoping to hear that I had a vision, a dream, or heard an audible voice that gave me specific instructions. But my answer was quite different. I told him that as I look back on the sequence of miraculous events that has brought me to the place where I am now, the hand of God and His divine orchestration are quite evident.

Today I preach to crowds of hundreds of thousands of people. I lead an international evangelistic ministry, and I have had the honor to lead more than ten million people to Jesus in our massive open-air evangelistic campaigns around the world. God never told me this was coming, and it never would have entered into my wildest dreams. But as I obeyed God's call one step at a time, His plan and purpose unfolded, layer by layer, with many confirmations along the way. I have found that this is usually the way God reveals His plan: one step at a time.

Jesus laid out a principle in Luke 16:10 that is absolutely essential in the quest to discover God's will for our lives. Jesus said, "He that is faithful in that which is least is faithful also in much: and he that is unjust in the least is unjust also in much." God calls us to small things before He calls us to great things. Many people want

God to speak audibly from heaven and give them direction, yet they aren't following the small directions they already have. If you aren't doing what you already know to do, why should God give you more instructions? If you aren't being faithful in the small things, why should God entrust you with more important things?

When you think about God's call and will for your life, don't think so much in terms of where you will eventually end up or what you will ultimately do. Instead think in terms of what God's will is for you right now! What is in your hand? What does He want from you today? As you follow Him in obedience, step by step and day by day, the picture will become clearer and He will entrust you with more and more. Eventually the day will come when you will look back on the many steps you took in faith and obedience, and you will see how the Lord carefully and strategically orchestrated each one in a way you never could have engineered in your own strength or wisdom.

Misconception #3: God Wants Everyone to Go Into Full-Time Ministry

I have often seen how people have experienced disasters in ministry because they felt the tugging of God's call on their lives and they misinterpreted that as being a call into full-time, fivefold vocational ministry. Even if you have an anointing to preach or teach, a strong desire to win the lost, or a unique charismatic ministry gift such as prophecy or healing, it does not necessarily mean God wants you to quit your job and start a church. As the apostle Paul had, I have the tendency to wish everyone were like I am, going to the nations and preaching the gospel full-time. But we must not forget that "each has his own special gift from God, one of this kind and one of another" (1 Cor. 7:7, AMP). If you venture outside the call and gift of God, you will not have the grace to do the job, and this could be disastrous for the one who has wrongly discerned God's call and all those unfortunate enough to wind up under his leadership.

I come from a long line of ministers. I am the fifth generation of preachers coming from my father's side of the family. My grandfather on my mother's side was also a pastor. My wife's father is also a pastor. Needless to say, I've been around a lot of ministry. I think a lot of people assumed that I went into the ministry because that is what was expected of me by my family, but it is quite the opposite. In fact, my father often counseled me by saying, "If you can do anything else—do it." In other words, if you can be happy doing something other than full-time ministry, you're probably not called to it. The truth is that occupational, fivefold ministry is not for everyone and should not be assumed without a clear and certain call. Yet many people who have not received the call to "ministry" still have a burning desire to serve the Lord. The good news is that serving God does not always mean becoming a preacher.

The kingdom of God needs ambassadors in every area of society. In Matthew 13 Jesus tells two stories with the same moral.

> Another parable put he forth unto them, saying, The kingdom of heaven is like to a grain of mustard seed, which a man took, and sowed in his field: which indeed is the least of all seeds: but when it is grown, it is the greatest among herbs, and becometh a tree, so that the birds of the air come and lodge in the branches thereof. Another parable spake he unto them; the kingdom of heaven is like unto leaven, which a woman took, and hid in three measures of meal, till the whole was leavened.
>
> —MATTHEW 13:31–33

The picture Jesus is painting through these two parables is clear. The kingdom of heaven is designed to grow, multiply, and infiltrate all that it comes in contact with, just as the small, seemingly insignificant mustard seed grows to become the greatest of the herbs in the garden, a tree large enough for birds to live in. And just as the small measure of leaven infiltrates every ounce of the lump of meal in which it has been hidden, in the same way God's kingdom is intended not to be confined behind the stained-glass windows of beautiful churches but to permeate the planet.

That can never happen if the only ones doing the work of the ministry are the apostles, prophets, pastors, teachers, and evangelists. Instead God's plan is for the real work of the ministry to be done by the plumbers, the high school teachers, the landscapers, the lawyers, and the doctors. We need men and women who carry the glory of God and the gospel witness into the White House, Hollywood, Wall Street, Main Street, and every other area of culture and society.

Through the years a fundamental disconnect has evolved between two parts of the church commonly known as the clergy and the laity. A hierarchical concept of ministry has evolved, which has segregated the two groups. This has resulted in a crippled system in which the career ministers, who are a minority of the church, have assumed the majority of the work of the ministry. Meanwhile the rest of the body of Christ, the majority, have been taught that they are not qualified for ministry and have been reduced to a crowd of spectators.

But when Ephesians 4 talks about the role of the apostles, prophets, pastors, teachers, and evangelists, the concept that emerges is very different from what has been modeled in the modern church. The New Testament pattern is for those in fivefold ministry offices to serve the body of Christ by equipping the saints for the work of the ministry (Eph. 4:12). If the body of Christ were compared to a football team, those in fivefold ministry would be the water boys, serving the team and helping to keep them equipped and refreshed.

The real ministers and ambassadors of God's kingdom to the world, the real players on the field, are the hundreds of millions of blood-washed saints who make up the body of Christ. What a tragic loss we have incurred by perpetuating the mentality that the few of us in fivefold ministry are the "real" ministers and the rest are just spectators.

My friend, God wants to use the gifts, talent, and calling He's given *you* to impact the world for His glory. Use whatever sphere of influence He places you in to further His kingdom and authority!

Preach Christ or Plant Corn

The brother of a famous evangelist, whom I'll call Sam, once jokingly explained why he became a farmer instead of an evangelist like his brother. He said that his brother was out in a field praying one day when the letters "PC" appeared in flames of fire across the sky. The brother said, "Lord, what does this mean?", to which the Lord replied, "Preach Christ!" Afterward Sam said he went out into that same field and "PC" again appeared in flames of fire across the sky. He asked the Lord, "Does this mean You are calling me to preach Christ?" The Lord replied, "No, Sam. I want you to *plant corn.*"

> God wants to use the gifts, talent, and calling that He's given *you* to impact the world for His glory.

Although this story was intended only to be a joke, there is a profound lesson here. Sam did not preach to multitudes as his brother did, but God did used him as a farmer. Because of his unique sphere of influence in the business world, he was able to share the gospel with people who might never have gone to hear his brother at a crusade.

Like these two men, some of us are called to be evangelists and others to become farmers, and God will use both for His glory. God calls some people to be used for His purposes in the business world. He calls other people to become teachers and others to be musicians. He is also calling people to work in sales, engineering, medicine, law, politics, and a myriad of other careers. God may call one to preach the gospel and the other to support him financially. They are both of equal value, and God will reward them both accordingly for

the different roles they played, if they are both obedient and faithful
to His call.

A heart doctor

A close friend of mind, Dr. Chauncey Crandall, is a nationally
known cardiologist in the United States. He is a man of science
and medicine and has achieved great success in his field of exper-
tise. But he uses his influence as a platform to advance the kingdom
of God. In his medical office he prays for his patients and shares
the love of Jesus with them. He truly cares about the hearts of his
patients—both the physical and the spiritual. Many times supernatural healings and miracles have taken place right in his office or in
the hospital. Today he is invited to speak about the miraculous from
the perspective of a medical doctor at conferences and conventions
around the world. His exceptional skills have given him a unique
sphere of influence where most preachers would never have cred-
ibility or a voice.

Spreading the gospel through business

Marie Green was the daughter of an evangelist and the wife of
a pastor. Her love for God was extraordinary, and it overflowed
in a generous heart for evangelism. She would crochet doilies and
sell them along with other things to raise money for missions. As
a mother of six children, three boys and three girls, she had a deep
desire to see her children grow up to serve the Lord and work for
His kingdom. The example she set left an indelible impression on all
six children, and they all went into the ministry, except one.

David was the "black sheep" of the family. He did not feel the
call to be a preacher, he had no desire to pastor a church or go to
the mission field, but what he did have was an affinity for math and
business. He took to the business world like a duck to water, and he
was good at it! But whenever he would get a promotion or achieve
some success, he did not receive the affirmation he desired from his
mother. She would say, "That's wonderful, David, but what are you

doing for the Lord?" This bothered him because he loved Jesus and wanted to serve Him, but God had not called him to preach.

In 1972 David opened a retail business called Hobby Lobby, and he began to discover God's will for his life. It did not happen overnight. In fact, he told me he did not know that serving God outside of the ministry was an option. But God began to unfold this great truth to him over time.

One day early in his career God spoke to David to give thirty thousand dollars to a particular ministry. Although he didn't have the money, he decided to find a way to be obedient; he gave what he could—seventy-five hundred dollars a month over the next four months. After he had given the money in obedience to the Lord, David discovered that the recipient of his donation had been on his knees praying for God's help at the very moment God had spoken to David about the need. He began to realize that his aptitude in business was not an insignificant coincidence; it was a gift God had given him for the spreading of the gospel! As the unfolding of God's will continued, he realized that his business did not belong to him at all—it belonged to God.

Today David Green is a billionaire. He has come to see that his business *is* his ministry, and he serves God in that arena faithfully together with his whole family. Hobby Lobby now has hundreds of stores that are located in forty-one states throughout America. Its vision statement says, "Hobby Lobby partners with organizations working to share the Good News of Jesus Christ to all the world." David Green and his family support ministries and world missions on a massive scale. Through their missions support they believe they have been able to reach more than one-third of the world's population with the gospel![2]

Not only does the Green family advance God's kingdom through financial giving, but they also see every aspect of their business as an opportunity to spread the gospel. They are fearless and uncompromising in their Christian witness. Hobby Lobby has a corporate chaplain, and Bible studies occur daily throughout their corporate complex. Hundreds of employees have given their hearts to Christ in the workplace, and David continues to see the gospel as the driving force behind his quest for success. David Green said, "Our organization wants to be remembered as one that knows the difference between temporal and eternal. Our business is only a means to an end and our end is to try to affect lives for eternity."[3]

David's mother, Marie, died in 1975, three years after Hobby Lobby had been founded. She never saw how her son, who had been the black sheep of the family, would go on to touch the ends of the earth with the gospel in a way that is historic. But I'm sure that today she smiles down from heaven to see that her son really did fulfill God's will for his life and has impacted eternity in a way that most preachers and ministers could only dream about.

Technicians for Jesus

Our ministry, Christ for all Nations, has conducted some of the largest evangelistic events in history. Tens of millions of people have received Jesus Christ as Savior during our campaigns. In fact, between the years 2000 and 2009 alone we counted more than fifty-three million registered decision cards from people who received Jesus Christ as their Savior! It is a historic harvest that is touching a continent in a profound way.

Most of the time when people think of the ministry of Christ for all Nations, they think of evangelist Reinhard Bonnke or myself—the preachers. But some of the most important people in our ministry work behind the scenes. One absolutely critical component to our mission is the technical team. These men who drive the trucks; set up the platform and lights; run the sound, the generators, and the cameras; and keep all the equipment running feel the same call to evangelism as the preachers, and they take their jobs just as seriously. Some have even given their lives as martyrs for the gospel. We salute them as the champions of the faith that they are!

One of my heroes is a man named Winfried Wentland. Today he

heads our technical team and has the extremely important responsibility of making sure all the equipment for the campaigns arrives in the right place at the right time. For more than thirty years Winfried has been driving our trucks across Africa. Crossing national borders, war zones, flooded rivers, and malaria-infested jungles, he has put his life on the line over and over again. Twelve times he was almost killed.

He has been shipwrecked and pulled from the bottom of a crocodile-infested river. He has been caught in the crossfire between rebel armies. He escaped from the hands of terrorists, robbers, child soldiers, and thugs. He has contracted malaria nearly two dozen times. Few people have had such adventures and heroic exploits for the gospel. However, Winfried says, "No one should or can do something like this out of a thirst for adventure, in search of a particular spiritual kick or a change of scene. This is not about personal satisfaction. To do this kind of work, apart from God's calling, you also need great perseverance. Most of the time it is just physically demanding, hard, dusty, routine work."[4] Winfried and the men who work alongside him are experts in their respective fields: engineering, electronics, logistics, etc. Although these vocations are not typically thought of as being associated with ministry, their work is absolutely vital to our mission. As a direct result of their efforts, literally tens of millions of Africans have heard the gospel and received Jesus Christ as their Savior.

Some people are called into full-time, fivefold, preaching ministry, and some are called to do a variety of other things. In reality, most Christians are called to serve God in "secular" spheres of influence. But one thing is certain: no matter what God calls you to do, it is for His glory and for the expansion of His kingdom.

Whether God calls you to full-time, vocational ministry or calls you to be His ambassador in the world of business, science, government, entertainment, or wherever, the principles are the same, the keys to discovering God's will are the same, the challenges and pitfalls are the same and, in the end, the reward will be the same. Contrary to what many people believe, God does not reward us based on how many people we lead to Jesus. He rewards us based on our obedience and faithfulness to His call and will. May you be faithful and obedient in whatever field He calls you to so that in the end you will hear those words, "Well done, thou good and faithful servant" (Matt. 25:21).

Chapter 3

HOW DO I RECOGNIZE GOD'S WILL?

A FARMER IN NORTH Carolina lived on a beautiful farm that his family owned for many decades. They had cultivated that same land for several generations, sowing and reaping in the fields year after year. Finally the farmer died, and after being in the family for more than two hundred years, the property was sold to one of the neighbors.

As the new owner of the farm was walking in the field, he saw a large, unusual-looking rock just barely sticking out of the dirt. He picked it up and began to examine it. He could immediately tell that this was no ordinary rock but some type of gemstone. He took it home, washed it, and took it to a jewelry store in the town where he lived. The jeweler confirmed what the owner already suspected; the old stone that had been in that field for thousands of years was a large, uncut emerald that has since proved to be worth several million dollars!

This gemstone was in that field all along just waiting for someone to come along and "discover" it. For generations farmer after farmer had worked in that field. Undoubtedly that emerald had been seen thousands of times before, but it was overlooked because, to the casual observer, it appeared to be nothing more than an ordinary rock.

This book is about discovering God's will for your life. When we "discover" a thing, we are actually uncovering or finding something that is already in existence but that we were unaware of previously. And while many people are desperately seeking God's will for their lives, the reality is that often what they are looking for is right under their nose, but they continue to look for it because they don't recognize it. In order to recognize a precious stone, one would need to be familiar with its characteristics and know what it should look like. In the same way, if we desire to discover God's will for our lives, we must learn to recognize the characteristics of His will.

GPS Gone Wild
Scan QR code

or visit
LiveBeforeYouDieBook.com/2

Characteristic #1: God Has a Standard Will and a Specific Will

I was approached recently by a man who wanted my advice in a very difficult situation. The man, who was a husband and father, had decided to leave his wife for another woman. He felt this other woman was his "soul mate," and he believed God had spoken to him and told him to divorce his wife to marry the other woman. When he asked me for counsel in this matter, I immediately knew God's will for the situation. I told him in no uncertain terms that it was absolutely *not* God's will for him to leave his wife for another woman and that God had *not* told him to do so.

Now you may ask, "How did you know this? Did you hear an audible voice from heaven? Did you receive a prophetic word?" No, I didn't even need to pray about it. I knew it was not God's will for this man to leave his wife and commit adultery (Matt. 5:28) simply because of what God has already revealed to us in His Word.

As we begin the journey of discovering God's will for our lives, it may seem like the options of tasks God may be calling us to are endless, and this can feel overwhelming. The good news is that God has already gone to great lengths to reveal to us in His Word what His will is for everyone—I call this the "standard will of God." But in addition to His standard will, God has something tailor-made for each of our lives. I call this the "specific will of God."

It is important, however, to understand that the specific will of God for your life will never go against His standard will—what He has already revealed to us in His Word. This understanding will quickly help us to sort through the plethora of options and instantly eliminate confusion. For instance, if you hear a voice telling you to open a Christian strip club or start a Christian drug cartel, you can be sure that the voice you are hearing is not from God.

These may be extreme examples, but this problem is not as far-fetched as you might think. It never ceases to amaze me the things that have been done throughout history by people who thought they were doing God's will when they were actually working in direct opposition to God's revealed Word. People claiming to be Christians doing God's will carried out the Crusades in the Middle Ages; the atrocities committed during that time could not have been more contrary to the teachings of Jesus. The Ku Klux Klan also uses the Bible to justify its detestable activity. According to Jesus these hateful hypocrites are murderers at heart. There are, in fact, many people who have done appalling things in the name of God. Many of them sincerely believed they were doing God's will. But there is no need for this confusion because God has clearly revealed His standard will for everyone in His Word if we would only make it our compass and our guide.

This book is mostly about discovering God's specific will for your life. This is something that is unique to you as an individual and something that you must discover for yourself. But our quest to discover God's will for our lives must begin with the Word of God. By following principles from the Scriptures, we will be able to navigate the ocean of options and opportunities without a shipwreck. Whatever you do in life, it must line up with God's Word, and He will *never* call you to do something that is contrary to it.

Characteristic #2: God Has a "Good Will" and a "Perfect Will"

God has a wonderful plan for our lives. But because God has given us the freedom to choose whether or not we are going to follow His will, it seems there are actually four possibilities for how we can respond to discovering God's will for our lives.

1. **We could be content to remain ignorant of God's will**. This is not you because if it were, you wouldn't be reading this book right now. You obviously have a deep desire in your heart to discover God's will for your life, and you are going to make that discovery.

2. **We could know what God wants us to do but choose to disobey Him and do things our own way instead.** This is disobedience, and it is the head-on collision of God's will and the stubborn rebellion of human flesh.

3. **We could know God's will and follow it in part but still settle for less than what God had in mind.** This is the biggest challenge most people face. You wouldn't be reading this book if you weren't interested in finding God's will. But settling for less than

God's best for our lives is often the easy road, and good things are often the greatest enemy of the best things.

4. **We can choose to contend for nothing less than God's best in our lives.** This is the big challenge for many people, because impatience to get what we want is a powerful force. But if we really believe God has a perfect will for us and that His will is always better than ours, we will be willing to wait for it and fight for it if necessary.

There is a perpetual conflict in the Christian life between what is "good" and what is "God." For example, I have seen Christians marry the wrong spouse because they were unwilling to wait for God to bring the right one along. God allowed them to do what they wanted and in some cases even turned bad situations around for His glory. Yet whenever we choose to disobey and do things our own way, something is lost that can never be restored. God will forgive and heal, but He will not turn back the hands of time.

I wonder sometimes if one day the Lord will show us what our lives would have been like and how He would have blessed us if only we had obeyed. A well-known poem written by an unknown author says:

> When I stand at the judgment seat of Christ,
>   and He shows me His plan for me—
> The plan of my life as it might have been
>   had He had His way—and I see
> How I blocked Him here, and checked Him there
>   and would not yield my will,
> Shall I see grief in my Savior's eyes;
>   grief, though He loves me still?
> He would have me rich, but I stand there poor,
>   stripped of all but His grace—

While my memory runs like a hunted thing,
　　down the paths I can't retrace.
Then my desolate heart will well nigh break
　　with tears that I cannot shed.
I'll cover my face with my empty hands
　　and bow my uncrowned head.
Now, Lord of the life that's left to me,
　　I yield it to Thy hand.
　　Take me, make me, mold me,
to the pattern Thou hast planned.[1]

God has a "good" will for your life, but He also has a "perfect" will. His perfect will and the blessings that accompany it are reserved for those who are willing to be radically obedient and to wait when necessary. Those who are slow to learn this lesson will make many trips around the wilderness and endure much unnecessary hurt and loss.

There are moments when God's way will seem so difficult, so prolonged, and so unrewarding, while our idea will seem much easier, much quicker, and so much more enjoyable. But it is only an illusion. Looking back, we will always find that God's plan is so much better than ours. There will never be an exception to this rule, so you might as well just decide from now on to yield to God's will, do it God's way, and wait for God's best.

Characteristic #3: God Often Calls Us to Do the Impossible

There are many books on the market today about self-improvement and personal success. They tell us that if we can learn how to exchange bad habits and attitudes for good ones, the end result will be wealth, health, fulfillment, and happiness. Many of the principles they teach are actually universal spiritual truths taken from the Word of God and then adapted to fit a wide variety of applications. They are like cheerleaders standing on the sidelines and chanting, "You can do it! You can do it!"

This is not one of those books. The content in these pages is not intended to challenge you to "grow," "develop," "achieve," or "change," but rather to yield your life to God. If the "You Can Do It" philosophy were true, we wouldn't need the Holy Spirit, would we? The "You Can Do It" mind-set needs to be replaced with another, which essentially says, "I *can't* do it on my own, but I can do all things *through Christ*. With His help and blessing anything is possible." Finding the will of God always requires faith for the impossible and a childlike dependence upon Him. The Bible is filled with the accounts of men and women who found their destiny in the perfect will of God by doing things that were impossible for them to do on their own.

Noah and his impossible project

Noah was commissioned to build a ship the size of an aircraft carrier by hand! The ark was an enormous boat, big enough to carry every kind of animal in advance of a global flood. Imagine the sheer impossibility of even building such a boat by hand, much less gathering all the animals. Yet Noah did it with God's help and grace. Engineers have studied the biblical dimensions of the ark and found that its design was perfectly proportioned for maximum sea-worthiness![2] Thousands of years ago the ark utilized principles of engineering and shipbuilding that have been discovered only recently. Noah would never have been able to calculate those things for himself, but God knew all along how to build the perfect boat. Noah just had to listen and obey. The people of Noah's day must have thought he had lost his mind as decade after decade he labored over this massive boat. But when the floodwaters began to rise, Noah was glad he had followed God's detailed instructions.

Abraham and his impossible promise

When Abraham was at an advanced age, God told him he was going to have as many descendents as the stars of the sky and the sands of the sea. How could such a thing be? He and his wife, Sarah, were much too old for that to happen. Yet Abraham believed in his heart that God was faithful and able to fulfill His promises. He did become the "father of many nations" just as the Lord had said, even though, from a purely natural biological standpoint, it was impossible.

Moses and his impossible passage

Moses was eighty years old when he stood before a bush ablaze with God's glory. God instructed him to bring approximately two million people out of Egypt and take them to a land He had promised to Abraham more than seven hundred years earlier. Moses had plenty of reasons to believe he was unfit for the job. He was too old. He was extremely shy. No one would listen to him. Pharaoh would probably kill him. Even if he were able to organize the people and even if Pharaoh allowed them to leave, how would he be able to lead and care for two million people in a hot desert without food and water? Yet despite these enormous obstacles Moses simply submitted to his destiny, obeyed to the best of his ability, and God did the rest! The story of God's faithfulness, provision, and protection in the Book of Exodus is one of the most remarkable accounts in the Bible.

Mary and her impossible pregnancy

A young girl named Mary was visited by the angel Gabriel and told that she had found great favor with God and had been chosen to give birth to the Messiah of Israel. But because she was still a virgin, she initially questioned how such a thing could happen. Still Mary submitted to the will of God, even though she did not fully understand it. As a result she fulfilled her destiny by giving birth to and raising God's Son.

The list of people in the Bible whom God called to do amazing things could go on and on. Throughout history God has always chosen very ordinary people to do very extraordinary things. Some were men while others were women. Some were young and others old. Some were well educated, and others were almost illiterate. But they all had something in common: they had all been called by God to be part of something

> God takes great pleasure in doing things through us that only He can do, so that in the end He receives all the glory, honor, and praise.

much bigger than themselves. Because of their willingness to simply yield themselves to the One who had created them and allow His purposes to be revealed in and through them, God used them in phenomenal ways. Healing evangelist Kathryn Kuhlman once said, "It isn't silver vessels that He's asking for. It isn't golden vessels that He needs. He just needs yielded vessels."[3]

It seems that one of the common characteristics of God's will is that it often calls us to do things that are impossible for us to do in our own strength. But as we yield our lives to Him, He causes His divine plans and dreams to become a reality! God takes great pleasure in doing things through us that only He can do, so that in the end He receives all the glory, honor, and praise.

Characteristic #4: There Are Times and Seasons in God's Will

As we are seeking the will of God, we can easily become frustrated if we don't understand that just as there are times and seasons in nature, there are also times and seasons in our lives and in the process of fulfilling God's will. This is what Paul was referring to when he said, "And let us not grow weary while doing good, for in due season we shall reap if we do not lose heart" (Gal. 6:9, NKJV).

Years ago a group of senior missionaries came together in a conference to discuss life principles they had discovered from several centuries of combined ministry experience. Their purpose was to be able to share this wealth of experience with succeeding generations. As these seasoned leaders shared their life stories, a familiar pattern began to emerge. They realized they had all experienced several common stages in their ministries, and they identified a fascinating five-step cyclical process that God had taken them all through. Here is a brief summary of what these veterans of the ministry discovered:

Stage One: The birth of the vision

Before anything tangible came into existence, these leaders had a vision that was imparted from the Holy Spirit. In its infancy the vision might have been very general with few obvious details about how it would actually be accomplished. But the vision was very real nonetheless and brought with it both a sense of excitement and an abiding awareness that it was from the Lord.

Stage Two: The place of preparation

Following the impartation of a vision into the hearts of these leaders came a time of preparation for the pursuit of that vision. Sometimes this season lasted for weeks. Sometimes this foundation-laying season lasted for months, and sometimes it required years. They also found that this was the stage when most of God's dreams for people are aborted because the individual refuses to do the necessary work. Many people have a vision given to them by the Lord. But a vision that is not embraced and nurtured through the appropriate season of preparation will invariably die. When God gives a vision, we must take some kind of action, or that vision will never become anything more than a fantasy.

Preparation may take many different forms. Sometimes the preparation involves a long, enduring season of prayer. Sometimes it involves an investment of time, money, education, and study. It may involve a time of serving someone else's vision or working for someone else to gain the benefit of experience. Failing to prepare properly will virtually assure failure at some point in the future.

Stage Three: The place of the wilderness and struggle

One of the biggest misconceptions about discovering the will of God is that if something is truly part of God's plan for you, there will be no struggle involved in accomplishing it. That is a myth! If God has called you to do something, you will almost certainly encounter a significant amount of struggle. God may actually even allow failures along the way, because He is more interested in the worker than He is the work. Sometimes God will even sacrifice a work to perfect a worker. This stage of struggle is the proving ground of faithfulness, and there is simply no substitute for it. (You can read more about the season of "wilderness" and struggle in chapter 16.)

Stage Four: The place of the realization of the vision

These leaders all found that the fourth step in the process was the place of realization or the attainment of the vision. This is the place we are all looking forward to, where we can finally enjoy the fruits of our diligent preparation and God's faithfulness.

Stage Five: The place of new beginnings and vision

This fifth stage was perhaps the most surprising discovery, because it was here that these leaders found themselves being challenged once more with fresh vision from the Holy Spirit. For some the vision was brand-new. For others it was to expand and enlarge the very thing God had originally given to them to do. These veterans found that the attainment of their dreams was not a destination but only another step in the cycle that continued to repeat itself throughout their lives. God would bring them back to the first stage of new vision, which would require more preparation and more struggle before the next level of realization would be attained.

These leaders came to the conclusion that their lives had been a continual cycle of ever-expanding vision. As God entrusted them with more, greater amounts of preparation were required, and the intensity of the battles they faced was always increasing.

Characteristic #5: God Is Interested in Our Journey, Not Just Our Destination

Why are we still here? Jesus died on the cross two thousand years ago and completed the work of salvation "once for all." So why doesn't He just rapture all of us so we can be with Him? One man told me that we are all just waiting for Jesus to build our mansions in heaven. I thought to myself, "It took Him only six days to create the entire universe. Can your mansion really be that difficult?"

If I were that guy and I thought my mansion in heaven was the only thing delaying the coming of the Lord, I would be praying, "Lord, forget the mansion. Just come and get me out of here!" And why wouldn't the omniscient God have thought ahead and had those mansions already prepared? There is obviously something else going on here. It seems clear that God is interested not only in our final destination but also in the journey because on that journey He does a work in our lives that has eternal value.

As a father of wonderful young children I can tell you that when kids get into a vehicle, they have only one thing on their minds—arriving at their destination. Five minutes into a five-hour road trip my kids will begin asking, "Are we there yet? Are we there yet? Are we there yet?" And the incessant inquiry will not abate until we have arrived.

This is how many of us are when it comes to God's will for our lives. We just want to get there already. We want to hear the little GPS unit say, "You have arrived." But in most cases there is a great deal of time that elapses between when God calls us and when we have fulfilled His will for our lives. What we need to understand is that the journey is an important process that matters very much to God. The process of following Him in obedience, step by step, through many unknowns, trials, and difficulties, is a significant part of our development and preparation.

One day a little boy happened upon a butterfly trying to break out of its cocoon. The little boy decided to help the struggling butterfly, but after tearing the cocoon open, he discovered that the butterfly inside was shriveled and weak—so frail, in fact, that it soon died. What the little boy did not realize is that pushing against the cocoon was a necessary part of the butterfly's development. Without the struggle the cocoon provided, the butterfly would not have the strength to survive when it emerged.

God uses the journey to teach us faith, to refine our character, and to equip us for the greater challenges that lie ahead. "If you have raced with men on foot and they have tired you out, then how can you compete with horses?" (Jer. 12:5, AMP). In most cases, without the journey, we would not be ready to step into the fullness of what God has for us. The journey is not just necessary for fulfilling God's will for our lives. It is in many ways an integral part of God's will for our lives.

> God is interested not only in our final destination but also in the journey, because on that journey He does a work in our lives that has eternal value.

In fact, even if you are in the process of seeking God's will right now, you are actually already fulfilling a part of it. God promises in Psalm 32:8 to "instruct thee and teach thee in the way which thou shalt go." My friend, don't make the mistake of thinking, even for a moment, that just because you don't know today what God's will is for your life that you are not making any progress. Something is happening right now. Your faith is being stretched, and your patience is being tried. Your spiritual ears are being tuned as you listen to hear the voice of God's Spirit. You are confronting doubts and questions. You may be going through a great struggle, but that struggle is all part of the process of birthing all God wants to do in your life. God *always* prepares us in advance for what He has in store for us! That process may be uncomfortable, but it is necessary nonetheless. Get ready. Good things are coming for you!

Chapter 4

WHAT IF GOD CALLS ME TO DO SOMETHING I DON'T WANT TO DO?

AS A LITTLE boy raised in the church, I was often confused by the words of certain songs. For instance, whenever the song "Bringing in the Sheaves" was sung, I thought we were singing about bringing in the "sheeps." I always wondered where we would get these "sheeps" and why we wanted to bring them in anyway. Spiritual themes, whether spoken or sung, can easily confuse the simple mind of a child, and while I learned quite early that "sheeps" is not even a word, the topic of God's will continued to be a point of confusion for a long time. I remember another song we used to sing, usually after a missionary had told depressing stories about the hardships and toils of the mission field:

> Jesus, use me. Oh Lord, don't refuse me;
> Surely there's a work that I must do.
> And even though it's humble, help my will to crumble,
> Though the cost be great, I'll work for You.[1]

As wonderful as those words are in and of themselves, there was something about the combination of the lyrics, the music, and the context that made me afraid of God's will for my life. I thought He must have something simply dreadful for me to do. I just knew He was going to send me deep into the jungle where I would live in a mud hut, survive on a diet of grubs, and wind up being eaten by cannibals. Looking back, my naïveté is quite amusing now, but the reality is that many people really are afraid to discover God's will for their lives, even if subconsciously. They think, "What if God wants me to do something I don't want to do?" "What if God wants me to do something I'm not good at?" "What if doing God's will means I have to give up my hopes and dreams?" I think sometimes people haven't discovered God's will simply because they are afraid to.

After I preached at a certain Bible college, one of the students approached me. He was nearing graduation and had been seeking God's will for many years but still had no direction. He said to me, "How can I figure out what God wants me to do with my life?" We were standing next to a lamp, and I noticed that it had been unplugged. I pointed to the plug lying on the ground and said to him, "How do you know what that three-pronged contraption is for? Should I stick it in my ear or use it to comb my hair?" He replied, "Of course not. It goes into the electric socket." How did he know that? Because of its shape. That plug fits so perfectly into that electric socket that there is no question that it was made for it. Even a child who had never seen a plug or socket before could figure out that they were made for each other.

This is one way you can know what God wants from you. Where do you fit? What do you enjoy? What brings you delight and satisfaction? I have heard people teach that God's will is always difficult and requires great sacrifice. But I have seen that the most effective people in any ministry, occupation, or just life in general are not the ones forcing themselves to do some dreadful task because they feel it is God's will. Rather it is the ones who are doing something they enjoy so much, they feel guilty taking a salary for it.

When you find something that makes you want to jump out of bed in the morning, when you find something that challenges and thrills you, when you find something that you sense you were made to do, chances are you are getting close to discovering God's will for your life. This does not mean that obedience, death to self, and sacrifice are never required or necessary. But when a person is doing what he was created to do, there is a taste of sweetness in the sacrifice, a sense of fulfillment in the obedience, and an enduring hope in the suffering.

If anyone ever knew what it was to suffer it was Paul the Apostle. In 2 Corinthians 11:23–28 he says he had suffered "in far more labors, in far more imprisonments, beaten times without number, often in danger of death. Five times I received from the Jews thirty-nine lashes. Three times I was beaten with rods, once I was stoned, three times I was shipwrecked, a night and a day I have spent in the deep. I have been on frequent journeys, in dangers from rivers, dangers from robbers, dangers from my countrymen, dangers from the Gentiles, dangers in the city, dangers in the wilderness, dangers on the sea, dangers among false brethren; I have been in labor and hardship, through many sleepless nights, in hunger and thirst, often without food, in cold and exposure. Apart from such external things, there is the daily pressure on me of concern for all the churches" (NAS).

Yet it was Paul who said, "I consider that the sufferings of this present time are not worthy to be compared with the glory that is to be revealed to us" (Rom. 8:18, NAS). And James even goes so far as to say, "Consider it pure joy, my brothers, whenever you face trials of many kinds" (James 1:2, NIV). How is it possible to have joy in the face of difficulties, trials, and suffering? It is possible because when we are in God's will, there is an unexplainable grace that accompanies us.

The Grace Comes With the Gift

Ephesians 4 is a fascinating chapter that will help us to understand how God's will and calling works.

- Verse 11 tells us about five of the callings God gives to men: "And he gave some, apostles; and some, prophets; and some, evangelists; and some, pastors and teachers."

- Verse 8 tells us where these callings came from: "When he [Jesus] ascended up on high, he led captivity captive, and gave gifts unto men."

- Verse 12 tells us why the callings were given: "For the perfecting of the saints, for the work of the ministry, for the edifying of the body of Christ."

- Verse 13 tells us what these callings will ultimately accomplish in the church: "Till we all come in the unity of the faith, and of the knowledge of the Son of God, unto a perfect man, unto the measure of the stature of the fulness of Christ."

Although we aspire to be like Jesus more and more, the truth is that none of us as individuals will ever attain to the full status of Christ's perfection or power in our mortal lives. But as a collective body not only can we attain to the measure of the stature of the fullness of Christ, but also we will! And God has given His church five gifts to help us reach that fullness: the apostles, prophets, pastors, evangelists, and teachers. You will notice that these five gifts that were given to mankind when Jesus ascended to heaven are not just random callings; they are five facets of Christ's own ministry. Jesus was the greatest apostle, prophet, pastor, teacher, and evangelist who ever lived, and when He ascended to heaven, He made provision for His agenda to continue on the earth by giving men and women the gifts needed to equip the saints to do the work of His ministry. According to Ephesians 4:13 the end result will be that the body of Christ (the people of God) will attain "unto the measure of the stature of the fulness of Christ." What a glorious destiny!

The reason these five ministry gifts are so important and so powerful is because of what we read in Ephesians 4:7: "But unto every one of us is given grace according to the measure of the gift of Christ." Grace comes with every gift! Jesus is the fullest expression of all of the five ministries, but when He ascended He distributed 20 percent of His ministry to the apostles, 20 percent to the prophets, 20 percent to the pastors, 20 percent to the teachers, and 20 percent to the evangelists. But not only did He give the gifts, He also gave grace according to the measure of the gift.

Did you ever receive some special gift for your birthday as a kid, then after you had torn open the package you realized it needed batteries to operate? When Jesus gives a gift, He also gives the batteries the gift requires to operate. The battery for "the gift of Christ" is grace. But He will give you only the measure of grace you need for the gift He has given.

I hear a lot of preachers talking about "burnout" these days, and it doesn't surprise me. Imagine a pure pastor who is wonderfully gifted in his pastoral office. He is using 100 percent of his God-given ministry gift, yet his gift is only

> Whenever God calls you to do something, He will always supply the perfect measure of grace so you will be able to operate in your gifting.

20 percent of what his congregation needs. This precious pastor is working around the clock, attempting to provide 100 percent of what the church requires to be perfected and edified in the way Ephesians 4:12 describes, yet he has only 20 percent of the grace to do that job! Anyone can see that this is a formula for disaster. If a person's body has only 20 percent functionality, we would say that person is handicapped. If an airplane lost all but 20 percent of its facilities, we would bring it in for an emergency landing. If a business operated at only 20 percent output, it would soon go bankrupt.

In Philippians 1 Paul is talking to his ministry partners (the ones who were supporting him financially). In verse 5 he expresses his gratitude for their partnership in the work of the gospel, and then in verse 7 he says, "Ye all are partakers of my grace." Do you realize that you can actually tap into the grace that is on someone else's life? By partnering with Paul's gift, the Ephesians became partakers of his grace! Let's go back to my example of the pastor who is burning out. Rather than attempting to provide 100 percent of his church's needs with 20 percent of the gift and grace, he should partner with others who are gifted in the areas he is not. When he partners with their gifts, he will also become a partaker in their grace, and the whole church will benefit.

The principle is simple but very profound, and Ephesians 4:7 encapsulates it: "But unto every one of us is given grace according to the measure of the gift of Christ." The grace comes with the gift!

> When God's gift and grace are resting on a person for a certain task or calling, he is able to do with joy what would seem difficult or even impossible to others.

Although this verse is set in the context of the fivefold ministry gifts, it is not just applicable to those called into "full-time ministry." The Bible says this grace is given to *every one of us* according to the measure of the gift of Christ. Whenever God calls you to do something, He will always supply the perfect measure of grace so you will be able to operate in your gifting. But whenever you try to operate outside your gift, you will find it difficult, burdensome, and miserable, because there will be no grace for it.

Take, for instance, someone who is called to live a celibate life. Paul the Apostle was one. In fact, he said in 1 Corinthians 7 that remaining single was a good thing, and he went so far as to say in verse 7, "I wish that all men were like I myself am [in this matter of self-control]. But each has his own special gift from God, one of this kind and one of another" (AMP). Although Paul preferred single-ness and wished everyone would remain single as he was, he had the wisdom to recognize that his ability to lead a happy and full life without a spouse was a special gift from God.

Paul understood that without the gift, there would be no grace. This is why Paul warned against those who would forbid marriage (1 Tim. 4:3). We have seen in the modern Roman Catholic Church priests who have been forbidden to marry, though many have neither the gift nor the grace to remain single. The result has been an appalling international scandal that has shamed Christianity and landed many priests behind bars. Paul's singleness was a gift, and with the gift God had given him the grace. Without the grace Paul would not have seen his singleness as a gift but as a burden.

There is also another interesting side note here. Because Paul was given the calling, the "gift," and the grace to lead a celibate life, he said, "I wish that all men were like I myself am." I have noticed that when the gift and grace are on a person's life to do something, it seems so natural and obvious to them, they think everyone else should be doing it as well. There are two lessons to learn from this principle.

First, don't make the mistake of trying to force those around you to do what God has called you to do, and don't look down on them for doing something other than what you think is so important. Recognize that, as Paul said, "Each has his own special gift from God, one of this kind and one of another" (1 Cor. 7:7, AMP). And second, if you think everyone should be doing one particular thing, chances are, that is what *you* are called to do! If you think everyone should be an evangelist, you are probably an evangelist. If you think everyone should be a political activist, then that is probably what God is calling you to do!

When God's gift and grace are resting on a person for a certain task or calling, he is able to do with joy what would seem difficult or even impossible to others. It is interesting that as a boy I dreaded the thought of being sent into the jungle in obedience to the call, but today I often go to the "jungle" preaching the gospel in Africa and around the world—and I don't know of anything I would rather do. I love my life, and I love my calling as a missionary-evangelist. What I had not taken into consideration as a child was this great truth: the grace comes with the gift, and the grace makes all the difference.

With this understanding, you never need to be afraid to discover God's will for your life. If He calls you to do something, He will also give you the grace to do it. When you are in God's will, covered by His grace, it is the most wonderful place to be in the whole world.

Chapter 5

WHAT IF I'VE ALREADY MISSED THE WILL OF GOD?

R EVELATION 13:8 DESCRIBES Jesus as the Lamb who was slain "from the foundation of the world." The implications of this verse are astounding. Before the fall of Adam and Eve in the Garden of Eden, indeed before the garden or its first inhabitants even existed, God had already initiated a plan of salvation that would culminate with the cross. This means that when Adam and Eve partook of the forbidden fruit, God was not surprised. Their failure had already been factored into His sovereign plan, and provision had already been made for redemption.

> If you are still breathing, it is not too late for God to intervene and restore what the locust and cankerworm have eaten.

If you have missed the will of God, be encouraged by this thought: Before God called you, before you were saved, in fact, before you were even born, God knew how your life would play out. Before you had made even one mistake, God took all your future failures into account, and in His infinite wisdom and love He preempted your blunders with a plan to turn your tragedy into a triumph in the end. With this knowledge you can be confident that if you are still breathing, it is never too late for God to intervene and restore what the locust and cankerworm have eaten.

Having said these things, it's important to understand that disobedience to God's will is not a trivial matter. God's grace does not guarantee that we will never have to live with negative consequences of our actions. Many times, even though God forgives and restores, there are still scars that remain from disobedience, and often the process of correcting our errant route is long and painful.

Jonah was called to go to Nineveh. The easiest, fastest, and most comfortable way would have been by ship. But because he disobeyed God's command, Jonah chose the hard way. Although he still ultimately made it to Nineveh, by the time he arrived he had been through a storm, thrown off a ship, and swallowed by a big fish. He spent three days inside that fish and was finally vomited onto the beach. Yes, Jonah made it to Nineveh all right, but the first option would definitely have been better. If you have missed the perfect will of God in your life, you need to take the following steps immediately.

Stop!

If you are going in the wrong direction, before you do anything else, you need to stop! As strange as it sounds, if we feel we have blown it, sometimes there is a temptation to just keep going. People who are trying to lose weight on a strict diet have struggled with this. They may have been very disciplined for a few weeks, but then a holiday comes. They ruin their diet for several days in a row, they gain a few pounds back, and rather than stopping the downward spiral, they say, "What's the use? I've already blown it. I might as well just give in." If you are still on the wrong track as you read this book, you need to realize that every day you continue on that path is a day you can never get back. Don't waste one more day or hour moving in the wrong direction. Stop *now*!

Acknowledge Your Mistake

Even if your mistake was not caused by deliberate disobedience against the known will of God, you need to acknowledge your mistake and ask for forgiveness. Maybe it is a job you shouldn't have taken. Maybe it was a bad investment or taking on debt that you ultimately realized you could not afford. It may have been something that happened as a result of carelessness or neglect, or it may have been caused by outright rebellion against God. Whatever the case may be, there is still redemption for everyone in the great grace and love of God. "If we confess our sins, He is faithful and righteous to forgive us our sins and to cleanse us from all unrighteousness" (1 John 1:9, NAS).

Repent

Repentance is such an often-misunderstood concept. Contrary to what many people think, repentance is not a dirty word. It's not just for the sinner who wants to get saved, nor is it just for those who are committing gross sins and living in blatant immorality. For the child of God repentance should be a lifestyle. To *repent* means to "turn," to change one's mind and direction. But here is where many people misunderstand. We tend to think of repentance as primarily turning away *from* something, as in turning away from sin and making a one-hundred-eighty-degree change to the opposite direction. But this is missing the real point. For example, a sinner could turn away from a sin and still be lost. In fact, there are many religions that teach morals and abstinence from various sins, but that in and of itself does not save anyone. Therefore, from the Christian perspective, what you turn away from is not really the issue. It is what you turn *to* that makes the difference.

If we think of repentance only as a one-hundred-eighty-degree turn, then we fail to understand that sometimes a minor but crucial fine-tuning is necessary to keep us calibrated with the heart of

God. If I am hiking through the wilderness and look at my compass and notice that I am only two degrees off course, I don't turn one hundred eighty degrees and go in the opposite direction, because if I did, I would still be going in the wrong direction! Instead my goal is to recalibrate myself so that I am once again moving toward my desired destination. If I am only two degrees off course, I still must turn, even if it is a slight adjustment, to align myself with the right direction. Repentance is the practice of the righteous. We must constantly turn our hearts to God—from darkness to light, from the flesh to the Spirit, from the temporal to the eternal, from death unto life.

With this understanding repentance takes on a whole new meaning. If I have lusted, lied, or stolen, if I have missed God's will because of disobedience, I must repent, yes. But I am not just repenting or turning away *from* those sins. I realize that those sins are actually a symptom of a deeper and more serious problem: that I am moving in a direction away from Christ. If there is sin in my heart or if I am not walking in God's will, it shows me that my heart is not toward Christ. I must refocus my heart and recalibrate it to point my whole being toward Christ. Sometimes repentance may have nothing to do with sin at all. It may simply be a slight correction in mind-set or attitude that brings our spirits back into alignment with the Spirit of God.

Turn to Jesus, and you will automatically turn from sin. Turn to Jesus, and you will always be facing in the right direction. If you have missed God's will, you need to stop moving in the wrong direction, acknowledge your mistake, and then get your heart realigned with Christ.

Start Afresh

I love Lamentations 3:22–23: "The LORD's lovingkindnesses indeed never cease, for His compassions never fail. They are new every morning; great is Your faithfulness" (NAS). God's mercy is truly an unfathomable wonder. Often we have a difficult time wrapping our minds around the scope of God's grace, but it is true—His mercy is new every morning! Every day is a new day. God is willing to forgive and offer us another chance every single day.

One of the most exciting developments of our day is GPS (global positioning satellite) technology. These amazing GPS devices have the capacity to navigate someone, with audible instructions, from wherever they are in the world to within a few feet of anywhere else on the globe they desire to be. One of the wonderful things about GPS devices is that they are full of grace and mercy. If the driver misses a turn, the GPS doesn't begin to scream, "You stupid idiot. I told you to turn. You missed it! That's it. Find your own way home. I quit!" It simply says in a calm voice, "Recalculating," and then begins to plot another course that will correct the mistake. I did hear of one person who, after having missed a turn, heard his GPS say, "Go straight ahead three hundred twenty-four miles and then turn right." Those kinds of instructions from a GPS are rare, but even if the driver had followed that unusual command, eventually the GPS would have gotten that person back to the place where he wanted to go.

> We cannot go back in time and undo things that have been done. But we can stop moving in the wrong direction, acknowledge our mistakes, repent, and then move on.

When we miss a turn in our negligence, ignorance, presumption, or rebellion, if we will stop, acknowledge our sin, ask for forgiveness, repent, and receive God's grace for a fresh start, we will hear the gentle and gracious voice of the Good Shepherd saying to our hearts, "Recalculating." He will then assign a new course that will get us back on track. It may take extra time and effort. It may be long and painful. It may even require that we "continue straight ahead three hundred twenty-four miles miles" before the next turn. But that turnaround will come if we keep following Him. God is a master at turning mourning into dancing and creating beauty from ashes.

Learn From the Past—but Don't Live in It

Some people live with terrible regret over the past. Everyone makes mistakes. Some of those mistakes may be the result of disobedience to the known will of God. But most are a result of a lack of prayer, a lack of wisdom, immaturity, impatience, or misunderstanding of the facts. If we could have known in the past what we know today, most of us would have made different decisions in some area of our lives. As the saying goes, "Hindsight is always 20/20." The reality is that we cannot go back in time and undo things that have been done. But what we can do, and must do, is stop moving in the wrong direction, acknowledge our mistakes, repent, and then move on.

When the Jewish authorities brought to Jesus a woman caught in the act of adultery, she was clearly guilty of the sin she was being accused of. Under the law adultery demanded death. Justice required that this woman pay the price for her sin. But Jesus had compassion on her. And after her accusers left, Jesus said, "'Woman, where are they? Did no one condemn you?' She said, 'No one, Lord.' And Jesus said, 'I do not condemn you, either. Go. From now on sin no more'" (John 8:10–11, NAS).

Although we are emotionally moved by this story, let me ask you a practical question. What gave Jesus the right to contradict the demands of the Law of Moses? Justice must be served and law-breakers must be punished. But you see, Jesus did not simply dismiss this woman's adultery as though it were unimportant. When He said these words, "I do not condemn you, either. Go. From now on sin no more," He was already on His way to the cross where He would pay for that woman's adultery with His own sinless blood. Justice would be served, and every debt would be paid.

My friend, if you have received forgiveness, your sins are washed and covered under the blood of Jesus. "As far as the east is from the west, so far has he removed our transgressions from us" (Ps. 103:12, NIV). "Therefore, there is now no condemnation for those who are in Christ Jesus" (Rom. 8:1, NIV). If ever anyone had a past to be ashamed of, it was Paul the Apostle, but this was his confession: "But one thing I do: forgetting what lies behind and reaching forward to what lies ahead, I press on toward the goal for the prize of the upward call of God in Christ Jesus" (Phil. 3:13–14, NAS).

There is a big difference between learning from the past and living in it. We need to learn from our mistakes lest we repeat them. But we cannot go back and change the past. What's done is done. We must move on with the remaining time we have and live from this moment forward in obedience to the will of God. To live in the past is to insult the spirit of grace and the sacrifice Jesus made on the cross. He paid the price so you could be forgiven from the mistakes of the past. If you have been washed in the blood of Jesus, God does not condemn you, and neither should you condemn yourself. Now, go and sin no more.

PART 2

FIVE SECRETS TO DISCOVERING GOD'S WILL

Chapter 6

SECRET #1—THE KINGDOM COMES FIRST

IMAGINE YOU ARE a member of the crew of an aircraft carrier in the US Navy. Like all the other crew members, you have been assigned a specific task. You might be a mechanic or a landing signal officer. You might have a prestigious position as a top gun fighter pilot or something as modest as a janitor. While the specific roles and functions will vary from person to person, every crew member is ultimately working toward the same objective: to fulfill the mission of that vessel.

In the military, depending on your position and rank, you may or may not be privy to the overall purpose for which your ship has been deployed, but in God's kingdom our commanding officer has made the ultimate objective clear, and if we keep this mission before our eyes, it will help us to discover and fulfill God's will for our lives. Regardless of the specific role we each are called to play, God's plan for our lives will always be aligned with the larger mission, and we can eliminate any initiative that is not in sync with it.

So what is God's supreme agenda in our world as revealed in Scripture? We need look no further than Jesus, who was in every way the complete and full expression of God's will in action. In the

Lord's Prayer Jesus prayed, "Your kingdom come. Your will be done on earth as it is in heaven" (Matt. 6:10, NKJV).

The prayer Jesus taught us to pray will one day be answered; God's kingdom will come, and His will shall be done on earth as it is in heaven! Let's fast-forward in time to see what this glorious fulfillment will look like. Consider the amazing words of 1 Corinthians 15:28: "And when all things shall be subdued unto him [Jesus], then shall the Son also himself be subject unto him that put all things under him, that God may be all in all." *That God may be all and in all.* What could be more complete than this? What could be more thorough than this? No more darkness; no more sin. Only righteousness in every corner of creation, God's will being done everywhere all the time.

> Regardless of the specific role we each are called to play, God's plan for our lives will always be aligned with the larger mission.

We see prophetic glimpses of this all throughout Scripture, even in the Old Testament. Isaiah and Habakkuk both declare, "The earth shall be full of the knowledge of the glory of the LORD, as the waters cover the sea" (Hab. 2:14; see also Isa. 11:9). A more thorough covering could not be articulated. It is a total and complete saturation.

The last chapter of the Bible paints a prophetic picture of what creation will ultimately look like. Revelation 21:4 says, "There shall be no more death, neither sorrow, nor crying, neither shall there be any more pain: for the former things are passed away." Isaiah 11:6 describes a time when wolves and lambs and leopards and goats will lie down together and be led by children.

Redemption has been the divine agenda since Adam and Eve fell in the Garden of Eden, and throughout human history God has been working diligently and unrelentingly to this end. Both Old and New Testament scriptures contain hundreds of references that run from start to finish in a seamless thread of single-minded intention.

In fact, according to Acts 3:21 every one of God's holy prophets since the beginning of the world has spoken about the restoration of all things. Those prophecies will be fulfilled, the prayer of Jesus will be answered, and God's kingdom will come. What a day that will be!

This is what we long for. This is what we pray for. This is what we work for—for God's kingdom to come and His will to be done on earth as it is in heaven! Regardless of what we do as an occupation, we all share a singular calling and mission in this life: to build God's kingdom on earth. This is why our "ship" has been deployed. This is the business we should all be investing in, and if we find ourselves moving in any other direction, we can be sure we are moving away from God's will for our lives.

The building of God's kingdom on earth is not just something we should keep in the back of our minds and try to contribute toward whenever an opportunity presents itself. Seeing God's kingdom come on earth must be our main ambition. In fact, Jesus said, "But seek *first* the kingdom of God and His righteousness, and all these things shall be added to you" (Matt. 6:33, NKJV, emphasis added).

For Such a Time as This

Perhaps the most well-known passage in the Book of Esther is in chapter 4, verse 14 where Esther's cousin and guardian, Mordecai, says to her, "And who knows but that you have come to the kingdom for such a time as this?" (AMP). Many exciting and uplifting messages have been based on this scripture. But often these inspirational sermons miss the point completely because they fail to take into consideration the true context of Mordecai's words. A close look at the circumstances surrounding this passage will show that Mordecai's message to Esther was not a feel-good, motivational speech, but rather a sobering and alarming ultimatum!

Esther was a young Jewish woman who was born into a broken family situation and was a minority in an oppressive society. The odds were against her right from the start. But almost overnight

Esther went from rags to riches, from poverty to the palace, and became the wife of King Xerxes I, making her one of the most powerful women in the history of the world. Irony seems to fill the pages of the Book of Esther. Just as Persia has unknowingly crowned a Jewish queen, the king's vizier, a man named Haman, is plotting a diabolical scheme to exterminate the Jewish race through a bloody massacre. There is only one Jew in the land who is in a position to intervene on behalf of her people. It is Esther.

It seems as though the pleasures of the palace had begun to intoxicate Esther. We see in chapter 4 that she begins to struggle with what course of action to take. As Esther looked around at the beautiful palace that was now her home and the luxuries, pleasures, conveniences, and wealth she had come to enjoy, it must have been difficult for her to imagine throwing it all away in some misguided attempt to be a heroine. She knew that taking this matter to the king would force her to risk everything she had, including her very life. Perhaps a more subtle approach would be best. Maybe she should just lay low and wait to see how things would play out. Perhaps at some point she would have an opportunity to put in a good word for the Jews without jeopardizing herself. After all, what good would she be to anyone if she were dead?

In Esther 4:13–14 Mordecai, sensing her internal struggle, sends this message to her: "Do not flatter yourself that you shall escape in the king's palace any more than all the other Jews. For if you keep silent at this time, relief and deliverance shall arise for the Jews from elsewhere, but you and your father's house will perish. And who knows but that you have come to the kingdom for such a time as this and for this very occasion?" (AMP). In other words, Mordecai said, "Esther, don't flatter yourself! You are not in the palace because you are so beautiful or wonderful or special. You have been placed in the position you are in because you are a strategic part of a divine purpose that is much larger than yourself. For you to stand up and speak out for your people is not some generous act of charity or an optional courtesy—it is the very reason God put you in the palace in the first place!" Mordecai went on to emphasize the severity of the situation, saying in essence, "If you try to protect your position at the expense of the divine purpose, God will replace you, and you will be destroyed!"

You might wonder what makes me think I can speculate about what was going on inside Esther's heart and mind. It is not only because of the context and the message Mordecai sends to her, but also because I see this scenario play out before my eyes every day in the West. Our comforts and conveniences have often made us complacent and indifferent to a dying world. We are often afraid to do anything that might disturb our cozy, pampered lives.

One man told me, "I can't talk about Jesus at work because if I do, I will lose my job." I've heard others say there are two topics they won't discuss at work: politics and religion. But the gospel is not an optional topic of conversation best left out of the workplace. On the contrary, you have that job because you are a strategic part of a divine purpose that is larger than you are. It is God who gave you your job, and He gave it to you for a reason. If you aren't willing to be a witness in your workplace, don't be surprised if God takes your job and gives it to someone who is unashamed of the gospel. God is calling you into the ministry—even if He positions you in a "secular" occupation. Your calling is to propel God's kingdom forward in whatever sphere you find yourself.

I've seen people drop hundreds of dollars at restaurants and on senseless entertainment, but when the offering plate goes around, they immediately begin to moan and complain. "All they do is ask for money in this church," they say. And when they do give a few dollars to the Lord, they feel they have been very generous. But the money in our bank accounts is not ours—it all belongs to God to begin with. He is not only the source of all our provision, but He is also the One who has given us the ability to create wealth. God hasn't blessed us so we can consume those resources on our own lusts and pleasures; He has blessed us so we can be a blessing. That is the reason we have those resources in the first place! If you aren't willing to bless God's kingdom with a cheerful heart, don't be surprised if He takes those means and gives them to someone who will be a good steward.

If God has entrusted you with money, you must realize that you are not the terminus; you are a channel through which those resources should flow. Yes, when water flows through a pipe, the pipe also gets wet! When God's blessings flow through you, you are also blessed personally, but never make the mistake of thinking you are blessed because you are so special or wonderful, intelligent or talented. As Mordecai said to Esther, "Don't flatter yourself!" You are not any better than the poorest beggar in the lowliest gutter. God has not blessed you because He loves you more than anyone else. He's blessed you for a purpose, and your fulfilling that purpose is not a side issue—it's the reason you have those blessings in the first place! If you won't do what God has called you to do, He will find someone else who will do it with joy!

If You Won't, Someone Else Will

Esau was the firstborn son in his family. He should have been his father's heir, the one who would carry on the family name and through whom God would fulfill His promise to Abraham. But Esau "despised his birthright" (Gen. 25:34). God passed over Esau because of his disregard and found in his younger brother a willing heart. Jacob inherited the destiny that should have been Esau's by birth and became one of Israel's greatest patriarchs.

Eli was the high priest, and his family had been called and anointed by God to serve Israel in the priestly office. But Eli's two sons had no regard for the Lord or His calling (1 Sam. 2:12). They desecrated the tabernacle, stole from the sacrificial offerings, and blasphemed God. They had a sense of entitlement and indispensability because they had been born into a family of power and privilege. But God tore the priestly calling away from them and from Eli's family and gave it to a young man named Samuel, who led the nation in their stead.

God chose Saul to be the first king of Israel. But he disobeyed the Lord and hardened his heart time and time again. Saul's children and grandchildren were destined to sit on the throne, but because of Saul's rebellion God cut his family off and instead anointed a young man named David through whose lineage the Messiah would eventually be born (1 Sam. 16:1–13).

Kathryn Kuhlman undoubtedly had one of the most influential ministries of the last century. She was a healing evangelist who witnessed extraordinary miracles and inspired many others to follow in her footsteps. But Kathryn said she was not God's first choice. She believed the Lord had called other people before her, but they had been unwilling to obey. She said, "I believe God's first choice for this ministry was a man, his second choice, too. But no man was willing to pay the price. I was just naïve enough to say, 'Take nothing, and use it.' And He has been doing that ever since."[1] Kathryn Kuhlman believed she received her mighty anointing and calling not because she was the best but because she was obedient.

Evangelist Reinhard Bonnke has preached to multiplied millions of people. Since 1987 our ministry, Christ for all Nations, which Evangelist Bonnke founded, has received more than sixty-seven million registered decision cards during our massive evangelistic campaigns around the world. It is truly one of the most remarkable ministry success stories of all time, and it is still continuing. But it wasn't always cake and ice cream. In his autobiography, *Living a Life of Fire*, Evangelist Bonnke tells many stories of the difficulties he faced, especially in the early years. His beginnings in Africa were humble. He often preached to small handfuls of people who were uninterested and did not want to respond to the gospel message.

The tide began to turn, however, when in four consecutive nights he received a prophetic dream in which he saw the continent of Africa being washed in the precious blood of Jesus, and he heard the voice of the Holy Spirit cry, "Africa shall be saved!" He took hold of that promise with all his might and began to move out in faith, but everyone did not welcome his ambition or enthusiasm. Provoked by jealousy, other missionaries began to complain to their denominational authorities that Reinhard Bonnke was able to exercise more freedom in his ministry than they were, and this prompted the missions board to order him, in writing, not to expand the ministry any further.

"My soul was smitten within me," he wrote, "as if I had been disowned by my own family. I had to...go off by myself in desperation. I needed to talk with God, and even more, I needed Him to talk to me." He decided to take a sabbatical to fast and pray. "I want to be at peace with my brothers," he pled. "I want to submit...and stop being driven by the burning vision You've given me of a blood-washed Africa." It was then that the Lord spoke to him words that shook him to the core. "Yes, you can do this," the Lord responded. "But if you drop My call, I will have to drop you, and I will have to look for someone else." That ultimatum was the only word he needed to hear. He immediately went home and wrote a letter of resignation to the mission board. "Let everyone else drop me," he prayed, "but, oh, Lord, don't You drop me."[2]

Had Evangelist Bonnke dropped the vision of a blood-washed Africa, God would have found someone else to reach that continent with the gospel. We often mistakenly feel we are indispensable, but the reality is that our failure to answer the call of God will not cause the purposes of God to fail. Rather it is the one who chooses to disobey who will suffer. God's plan will still come to pass, even if He has to raise up someone else to fulfill it.

John the Baptist gave a sobering warning to the Jewish leadership of his day. He knew that, as part of God's chosen people, they felt superior to other races and had a sense of indispensability. But in Matthew 3:9 John says, "Do not suppose that you can say to yourselves, 'We have Abraham for our father'; for I say to you that from these stones God is able to raise up children to Abraham" (NAS). God is able to raise up the next world changer overnight. He can take someone from the gutter, like Esther, who was a "nobody," and put her in the palace—and He needs no one's permission.

Mordecai told Esther essentially, "God's purposes will come to pass one way or another, with or without you." But his warning became even more severe. Mordecai went on to tell Esther, "For if you keep silent at this time, relief and deliverance shall arise for the Jews from elsewhere, but you

> Propelling God's kingdom forward is not a side issue—it is *the* reason you were saved, it's *the* reason you were born.

and your father's house will perish" (Esther 4:14, AMP). God's purposes are like a freight train that cannot be stopped, and the most dangerous place in the world to stand is in the way of those purposes because they will not slow down to avoid running over you. If you doubt this, just ask Pharaoh, who refused to let the children of Israel go in the Book of Exodus. God has absolutely no chance of losing. We are the only ones who stand to lose when we fail to obey.

My friend, we have been placed in this world for a purpose: to propel God's kingdom forward. This is more than a preference or privilege; it is a divine responsibility and duty for which we will be held eternally accountable. Propelling God's kingdom forward is not a side issue—it is *the* reason you were saved, it's *the* reason you were born. You have come into the kingdom for such a time as this!

Meaningless! Meaningless!

Notice that Matthew 6:33 says if you will seek the kingdom of God first, "all these things shall be added unto you." The Greek word translated *added* is a mathematical term. From a perspective of real value, addition is meaningless unless we are dealing with numbers greater than zero: $0 + 0 = 0$. This is true ad infinitum. One could add zeros together until they stretch around the globe, and still the value of all those added zeros would be zero. Zero is the ultimate value of all of the accessories we seek in life. The writer of Ecclesiastes said it best:

> "Meaningless! Meaningless!" says the Teacher. "Utterly meaningless! Everything is meaningless." What does man gain from all his labors at which he toils under the sun? Generations come and generations go, but the earth remains forever. The sun rises and the sun sets, and hurries back to where it rises. The wind blows to the south and turns to the north; round and round it goes, ever returning on its course. All streams flow into the sea, yet the sea is never full. To the place the streams come from, there they return again. All things are wearisome, more than one can say.
>
> —ECCLESIASTES 1:2–8, NIV

The Lord told Isaiah to cry out and to prophesy these words that still ring like an anthem to our world that chases feverishly after possessions, glory, and gratification.

> A voice says, Cry [prophesy]! And I said, What shall I cry? [The voice answered, Proclaim:] All flesh is as frail as grass, and all that makes it attractive...is transitory, like the flower of the field. The grass withers, the flower fades, when the breath of the Lord blows upon it; surely [all] the people are like grass...Behold, the nations are like a drop from a bucket and are counted as small dust on the scales....All the nations are as nothing before Him; they are regarded by Him as less than nothing and emptiness (waste, futility, and worthlessness).
>
> —ISAIAH 40:6–7, 15, 17, AMP

Movie stars, world leaders, and business tycoons all think they are very important, and nightly news reports would have us believe the world revolves around these people and their influence, power, and wealth. But from God's perspective it is all nothingness and futility. All of their wars, struggles, and efforts to rise to the top of the ladder are all worthless. And if this is so for the most powerful people, how much more for us? When all is said and done, what is the purpose of everything we do? We struggle and toil all our lives, pushing, striving toward something, some purpose, but what?

In an attempt to find meaning, we tell ourselves that we are doing it all for our children, but what do we teach our children? From us they learn to add zeros together, and thus they inherit the same meaningless futility with which we have lived. All the goods we acquire soon rot, precious moments are forgotten, and money evaporates as the dew. The world keeps spinning and changing as people and kingdoms come and go. The wise will see that "the Teacher" was right—everything in this world is utterly meaningless and has less value than a zero. Yet people spend their entire lives adding these meaningless zeros together.

But when we are seeking first the kingdom of God, it means we have made God's kingdom the priority in our lives. And when God's kingdom is number one, suddenly all the zeros after it have meaning: 10; 100; 1,000; 10,000; 100,000; 1,000,000! All the zeros of life are meaningless unless God's kingdom is first! But put God's kingdom first, and not only will you find ultimate purpose and meaning in life, but also even the small things will also take on significance.

I come from a long line of preachers of the gospel—five generations on my father's side. It all started with my great-great-grandfather, August Kolenda. One day as I was studying our family tree, it occurred to me that we know much about Great-Great-Grandpa August and the generations of men of God who followed him, but we know almost nothing about all the previous generations of unsaved ancestors who came before him. It's as though before Jesus came into the Kolenda family, nothing mattered. The stories, the struggles, the victories, the details just don't matter to anyone.

Before Jesus came into the Kolenda family, everything was meaningless and worthless—just a bunch of zeros. But that night when Great-Great-Grandpa August heard beautiful music coming from a church, went inside and sat down on the back row, heard the gospel, and made a decision to live for God's kingdom, suddenly something of value entered into our family. In front of all the meaningless zeros God's kingdom became number one, and since that day all the blessings that have been added to our family have become a glorious and wonderful heritage that is worth more than great riches.

The Taylor brothers were both highly ambitious. Both wanted to make a difference. Both wanted their lives to count. The older brother decided to bring honor to the family name by pursuing a prestigious political career. The younger brother decided to dedicate his life to preaching the gospel and went to China as a missionary. Contemporaries of the Taylor brothers would have certainly seen the older brother as the more successful one, but today he is virtually unknown except for his relation to his younger brother, Hudson. Hudson Taylor became one of the most well-known pioneer missionaries in history, and he is loved and honored around the world today. One brother sought fame, fortune, and power. His reputation, money, and influence have long since taken flight on the wings of time. The other brother seemed to throw his life away serving God in a distant land. But the legacy of Hudson Taylor lives on because, though he was not a millionaire, a superstar, or a world leader, he gave his little life to something eternal.[3]

The missionary martyr Nate Saint once said, "People who do not know the Lord ask why in the world we waste our lives as missionaries. They forget that they too are expending their lives...and when the bubble has burst, they will have nothing of eternal significance to show for the years they have wasted."[4] Christianity is counter intuitive. It is a paradox and preaches a message that is exactly opposite the world's wisdom. The world says, "Protect your life if you want to save it." Jesus says, "For whoever wishes to save his life will lose it;

but whoever loses his life for My sake will find it" (Matt. 16:25, NAS). Solomon, one of the wealthiest and most powerful kings who ever lived, tasted all the world had to offer and came to the conclusion that it is all "meaningless." It is just as the apostle John wrote, "The world passeth away, and the lust thereof: but he that doeth the will of God abideth for ever" (1 John 2:17).

Am I trying to convince you to become a missionary? Not at all. Whenever "God's will" is mentioned, people automatically begin to think of quitting their jobs and going into "the ministry." It is so unfortunate that the body of Christ has often been dismembered by class distinctions between "clergy" and "laity." Those in full-time, occupational ministry have been put on pedestals and are expected to be the ones advancing and representing the kingdom of God while the "normal" Christians are busy with secular enterprises. For many Christians their "faith" is a Sunday morning matter, just one of life's many associations discreetly acknowledged on their personal profile next to political party affiliation and favorite sports teams.

But in Christianity there are no distinctions or classes. We are all a part of the priesthood, and we are all expected to be about kingdom business. God wants your life to be an annexation of His kingdom on the earth! He wants you to be an ambassador for His kingdom wherever you go and whatever you do. In that sense we are all called to be in "the ministry."

All These Things

Careers, life partners, finances, location, and education should never be our chief focus. All of these things will be sorted out and added to us as we keep the kingdom of God as our primary concern. As we seek God's will for our lives, we can be sure that it will *never* move us in a direction that is contrary to God's kingdom purposes.

The imperative of seeking God's kingdom is not only relevant in the context of highly spiritual ministry issues. Jesus says that if we seek the kingdom first, *all these things* will be added to us. This is one of the most powerful secrets to discovering God's will for your life. If you will set your sights on His kingdom and make that your priority, as you move toward it you will automatically come across everything else you need!

Once after I had finished preaching about the kingdom of God, an elder in the church approached me and said, "You know, all these lofty ideas are wonderful, but most of the people in the church are just trying to figure out how to pay their bills and get along with their spouse and raise their kids and do a good job at work." I realized that in many ways this dear friend was right. Most Christians consider the kingdom of God to be something so lofty that it is best left to pastors and evangelists.

The famous psychologist Abraham Maslow espoused a similar view. He constructed a pyramid that he titled the "Hierarchy of Needs." It was his opinion that before someone could "self-actualize," he first needed to meet the baser needs of human nature such as food, shelter, and companionship. Maslow believed that before one could reach the lofty ideals at the top of the pyramid, he would need to climb from the bottom, meeting the basic needs first.[5] This seems to be the most intuitive approach to life. Many people think the kingdom of God is an ethereal and irrelevant topic, and they prefer to be "down to earth." They have decided to first concentrate on putting food on the table and paying the bills. This seems to be the responsible and practical thing to do.

But what Jesus taught is quite the opposite. Jesus said, "Don't worry about what you will eat or what you will wear. Your Father in heaven knows you need these things, and He will take care of you. Instead seek first the kingdom of God, and all these things will be added to you." (See Matthew 6:25–33.) What Jesus was teaching was Maslow's Hierarchy of Needs in reverse. Jesus turns Maslow's pyramid upside down! Jesus teaches us to start at the pinnacle of the pyramid, the highest and loftiest place. Put the kingdom of God first, and *everything* else will be taken care of—physical, mental, and emotional needs included.

- If you want to know what job God has for you—seek His kingdom, and you'll find your occupational calling!

- If you want to know whom you should marry—seek His kingdom, and you'll find your spouse!

- If you want to know where you should go to college—seek His kingdom, and you'll land in the right school!

- If you want to know where you should live—seek His kingdom, and He'll lead you to the right geographical location!

Can it really be that simple? Could this one command really be the secret to finding out God's will? My friend, these are not my words. These are not the words of a philosopher or a preacher. These are the words of the Son of God Himself; "But seek *first* the kingdom of God and His righteousness, and all these things shall be added to you" (Matt. 6:33, NKJV, emphasis added).

I am an evangelist who travels the world preaching the gospel. The work I do would have been impossible without my amazing wife, who shares my passion for evangelism and ministry. I know many preachers whose ministries have been cut short because they married the wrong woman, but I am so thankful that the Lord gave me a wife who is a perfect fit for the calling on my life. You might think I had to search high and low to find such a wonderful wife. The truth is that I wasn't even looking for a wife when I met her. I was actually in Bible school in obedience to the call of God. My heart was set on serving the Lord. I was seeking God's kingdom, and then one day it happened—I fell in love! As I was seeking God's kingdom, He gave me a wife. I think this is how we often discover

God's will for our lives. As we follow Him daily, He "adds" unto us blessing after blessing, and every need we have—be it emotional, physical, financial, or spiritual—is taken care of.

Many people have put education first in their lives. When all is said and done, they will be highly intelligent fools, missing the greatest wisdom of all in their endless search for knowledge. Many people have put money first in their lives. When all is said and done, they will know the truth of Matthew 6:24: "You cannot serve both God and Money" (NIV). Many people put family first in their lives. When all is said and done, it is their family who will pay the price for their misdirected priorities. When we put anything ahead of Christ and His kingdom in our lives, not only will we miss God's kingdom, but we will also miss all the other treasures as well.

We Seek the Kingdom Because We Love the King

A word of caution and clarification is due at this point because there are many people who have misconstrued and terribly misunderstood Jesus's promise. They view Christ and His kingdom as a means to an end, a tool to get what they want in life. They have come to Jesus because they see Him as a way to become healthy, wealthy, and wise. They have believed a humanistic version of the gospel that emphasizes the last word of Matthew 6:33: "All these things shall be added unto *you*." Although there are wonderful fringe benefits to serving God, if those benefits become our motivation, we have missed the point completely.

God is not looking for spiritual "gold diggers" who use Him and His kingdom to get rich, or to become popular or powerful. On the contrary, God is looking for people whose eyes are so fastened on Him and Him alone that none of the peripheral attractions are even in view. It is those with consecrated hearts to whom He says, "Don't worry. I'll take care of everything else you need."

Although seeking God's kingdom first will give us fulfillment and purpose in life, we do not seek God's kingdom primarily for the sake of becoming self-actualized or having a sense of accomplishment. It's true that as we seek God's kingdom, our material and financial needs will be met, but we do not seek God's kingdom primarily because of the monetary benefits. It is obvious that seeking God's kingdom results in eternal rewards that are very literally "out of this world." But we do not seek God's kingdom primarily to win an eternal prize. We do not seek the kingdom because we love its benefits—we seek the kingdom because we love its King! When our love for the King becomes our paramount incentive, then and only then do we have things in the right order.

Building the kingdom of God must be our primary objective in life, but the underlying motivation must be love for the King. The only way a person can be truly committed to the kingdom of God is to be consumed with love for Christ. If we are driven by a philosophy or an ideology, a desire to make the world a better place or to see a new order established, then our ambition falls into the same category as communism, Marxism, socialism, and all the other "-isms." Seeking the kingdom of God is in a category all by itself because it stems from a fountain deeper than any motive in this world—divine, supernatural love for the King. This love is the foundation and the driving force behind the kingdom that will endure long after all others have crumbled to dust.

Chapter 7

SECRET #2—THE SURRENDERED WILL

L ET'S APPROACH THE Garden of Gethsemane now with reverence and awe. Listen to those timeless words that fall from trembling lips, "Father, if thou be willing, remove this cup from me: nevertheless not my will, but thine, be done" (Luke 22:42). I think we often overlook the significance of what happened in Gethsemane, but as it relates to our redemption nothing could be more important. If Calvary is the door to salvation, Gethsemane was the hinge. It was here in this garden where the eternal future of humanity hung in the balance. It was here that our fate was decided. All of history was depending on this moment.

Where Adam failed in the Garden of Eden, Jesus prevailed in the Garden of Gethsemane. And the key to Christ's victory here was the secret of His whole life, embodied in those seven immortal words, "Not my will, but thine, be done." The Roman soldiers seized Jesus and crucified Him, but they could not take His life, for He had already laid it down in Gethsemane. "No one takes My life from Me," was Jesus's confession, "but I lay it down of Myself." You cannot kill a man who is already dead! It is here that we find the next great secret for discovering God's will for our lives—the secret of the surrendered will.

We must begin by recognizing something so simple yet so significant: there may be a difference between what we want and what God wants. With this awareness we must constantly make sure our will is surrendered to His. Many times people embark on the journey to discover God's will having already made up their minds about what they think God wants them to do. And often what they are actually seeking is divine validation of what they desire. If you truly want God's will for your life, you cannot simply pray, "Your will be done." You must include, "Not my will."

In the last chapter we discussed the first secret to discovering God's will, which is to seek the kingdom first. And we studied the Lord's Prayer, in which Jesus taught us to pray for God's kingdom to come. In this chapter I would like to emphasize the second part of the same sentence in the Lord's Prayer we focused on previously. Jesus prayed, "Thy kingdom come," and with the same breath continued His petition by saying, "Thy will be done" (Matt. 6:10). Those phrases may seem to address two completely separate topics, but they actually go hand in hand. In fact, you can't have one without the other.

To understand the correlation between God's kingdom coming and His will being done, let us first consider what a kingdom is. In ancient times kings ruled their kingdoms with absolute sovereignty, and their word was law. A kingdom was the realm in which a certain king's authority and will were recognized and obeyed. Let's take a more contemporary kingdom, the British Empire, for example. The American colonies were at one time under the rule of the king of England, and for this reason he was able to collect taxes from the colonists. Even though the king was separated from these American subjects by a great distance

> If you truly want God's will for your life, you cannot simply pray, "Your will be done." You must include, "Not my will."

geographically, they were a part of his kingdom because they were under his rule. But when the American colonists rebelled and won independence from the empire, they no longer obeyed the wishes of the British king. His will was no longer their concern, because they weren't a part of his kingdom and therefore not under his authority.

There are many people who for some reason think that whenever the Bible talks about the kingdom of God, it is referring to "heaven." But when Jesus taught about the kingdom of God, I think He had something more in mind. If a king's kingdom is the realm in which his will is observed and obeyed, then the kingdom of God is present wherever God's authority is acknowledged and submitted to. Therefore, when Jesus prays, "Your kingdom come," He is inferring what He states explicitly in His next breath, "Your will be done."

But the prayer of Jesus is not like Burger King's motto. Jesus isn't saying, "Father, have it Your way as everyone else has it their way." Jesus was praying for God's will to be done *exclusively*—the way it is done in heaven. In other words, all other wills bow to the divine will, God's authority is recognized and submitted to, and everything comes into alignment with what the Father desires.

The Kingdom "in Earth"

I love the way the Lord's Prayer is rendered in the King James Version. Jesus prayed, "Thy kingdom come, Thy will be done in earth, as it is in heaven." While some translations say, "Your will be done *on* the earth," the King James says, "Thy will be done *in* earth." Genesis 2:7 says, "God formed man of the dust of the ground." We are made from the earth, we are vessels of "earth," and when God's will is done in us, or "in earth," then and only then can God's will be done "on the earth."

Jesus prayed, "Thy kingdom come," and continued by saying, "Thy will be done." These are two inseparable conditions. Wherever God's kingdom has come, there His will is being done. Likewise, when God's will is being done, there His kingdom has come. If we are seeking the kingdom first, then the kingdom is our main ambition, and this is demonstrated in two ways. First, we want to see God's will done "*in* earth" (in our own lives), and second, we seek to see His will done *on* the earth (in the whole world).

> If you want to see God's kingdom come *on* earth, it starts with God's will being done *in* earth—in you!

It all begins with the heart—it all begins with us. Many people want to change the world. They want to see the nations bow their knees to the King of kings and the Lord of lords. Yet the hearts and lives of many of these people still aren't surrendered. Jesus said, "The kingdom of God is within you" (Luke 17:21, NKJV). What was Jesus talking about? He was talking about God's will being done in the hearts of men. Human kings fight over land and spoil, but the real estate God desires is that of the heart.

Jesus said in John 7:38, "He who believes in Me, as the Scripture said, 'From his innermost being will flow rivers of living water'" (NAS). He didn't say we would see rivers of water flow from heaven— He said they would flow from inside His people! God's kingdom is not coming out of the blue sky; it's coming from within us! God's will is that every believer becomes an annexation of His kingdom, a portal through which He can pour His glory and release His power into the world. If you want to see God's kingdom come *on* earth, it starts with God's will being done *in* earth—in you!

Romans 14:17 says, "For the kingdom of God is not meat and drink; but righteousness, and peace, and joy in the Holy Ghost." This is the inward condition of people who have submitted themselves to God. They are filled with righteousness, peace, and joy in the Holy Ghost! It's heaven *in* earth!

The Valley of Brokenness

Years ago I had a vision in which I saw a dam. On one side was a mighty river, but on the other side was dry, cracked earth. I understood that the river represented the glory of God and the dry ground represented the world. I knew intuitively that the river was supposed to flood the dry ground, as the Scriptures say, "For the earth shall be filled with the knowledge of the glory of the LORD, as the waters cover the sea" (Hab. 2:14). But the dam's mighty wall seemed impenetrable. Suddenly I saw something else. Tiny cracks began to form in the wall, and razor sharp spurts of water were shooting out of these broken places. Soon larger and larger chunks of the wall began to fall away until water was pouring in from all sides. Suddenly in one moment the entire wall was swept away, and the river flooded the dry ground, leaving no place untouched.

I knew instinctively that those cracks in the wall represented "broken" men and women. They are those who have surrendered their lives to God, praying with Jesus, "Not my will, but thine, be done." Suddenly I knew how the glory of the Lord would cover the earth as the waters cover the sea. In fact, it is through these people that, even now, the kingdom of God is invading the fallen world. God's eternal glory will penetrate the natural world through broken men and women. And when the kingdom of God comes into contact with the fallen world, we begin to see heavenly effects: the sick are healed, the dead are raised, bondages are broken, and the supernatural begins to happen.

This is exactly what Jesus demonstrated when He was on earth. "Not my will, but thine, be done" was not just a prayer Jesus prayed one time before His crucifixion. This was the unvarying posture of His heart. He was always living and walking in perfect submission to the will of God. Everywhere Jesus went, He taught about the kingdom, but He didn't just talk about it, He demonstrated it!

First, the kingdom was inside of Him because He was perfectly submitted to His Father's will. And consequently the kingdom was manifest wherever He went: the sick were healed, the dead were raised, and demons fled. "Thy will be done in earth, as it is in heaven" was not Jesus's hopeful musing for an imaginary utopia.

Jesus fulfilled His own prayer and showed us how it will be answered. Through Jesus God's will *was* being done on earth as it is in heaven, and this is what God desires to do through our lives as well. But it all begins when we come to a place where our will is submitted to God's—"Not my will, but Yours, be done." It is in this place of submission that we will discover and fulfill God's will for our lives.

The Greek term *seek* is an action word. It is ongoing and continuous. This is important to understand because discovering God's will for our lives is not simply a destination to be reached; it is a posture of the heart! It is not simply a matter of choosing the right career path or marrying the right spouse. It is an ongoing stance of submission to God's will above our own. It is a lifelong prayer, "Not my will, but thine, be done." As long as we live, we must continue to follow and obey. Discovering God's will for our lives happens daily as we constantly and faithfully seek to know and to do His will.

As we travel on the journey of discovering God's will, the narrow road cuts through a dark valley where God tests our hearts and breaks us. The breaking process is uncomfortable but very important to endure if we want to see God's will done in our lives. The valley of brokenness is where we learn to say, "Not my will, but Yours, be done." This brokenness, while painful, releases amazing power and makes us useful to God.

When a cowboy wants to harness the potential of a beautiful and powerful stallion, he sits on the horse's back. This is very uncomfortable to the animal. It has always been its own master. It has always done what it wanted to do. And when the cowboy begins to exert his will over the horse's, a desperate struggle ensues. The horse begins to kick and thrash and buck in an attempt to throw the cowboy off its back. But the trainer will keep getting back on the horse and keep riding it until it stops kicking and bucking. The cowboy knows that until the horse's will is broken, it is of little use. So it is with God's people. Until we are broken, we are of little use to God's kingdom.

When God told Gideon he would become a mighty deliverer of

Israel—and Gideon finally believed Him—the once fearful warrior may have pictured himself riding on a noble steed, commanding a legion of soldiers in glorious battle array. But God had something very different in mind. Gideon would not have a legion of warriors at his command, only a ragtag gang of three hundred roughnecks. There were no archers, no cavalry, and no infantry. They were not outfitted with the latest battle equipment: no swords, shields, or spears. Instead they carried curious trumpets and jars of clay. Finally the moment came for Gideon and his men to face the innumerable hordes of the Midianite army. In obedience to God's command they broke their jars of clay, in which were hidden fiery torches. They blew their trumpets and began to shout. The Bible says the Midianites were thrown into confusion, and Israel won an unlikely victory. (See Judges 7.)

Paul, speaking about the power of God, says in 2 Corinthians 4:7, "But we have this treasure in jars of clay to show that this all-surpassing power is from God and not from us" (NIV). Before the great power that is inside us can be unleashed, we must be broken like Gideon's clay jars.

When Gideon defeated Midian with a handful of motley soldiers carrying clay jars and trumpets, it was obvious that the victory could have come only from God Himself, and all the glory went to Him. So it is with our lives. When we are broken vessels of clay, then God's power shines out, and all the glory is His. This is why Paul says, "But God has chosen the foolish things of the world to shame the wise, and God has chosen the weak things of the world to shame the things which are strong, and the base things of the world and the despised God has chosen, the things that are not, so that He may nullify the things that are, so that no man may boast before God...that, just as it is written, 'Let him who boasts, boast in the Lord'" (1 Cor. 1:27–29, 31, NAS). God loves to use broken vessels because through them He gets the most glory!

In Matthew 14 we read an amazing story about a miracle where

Jesus fed a multitude with a just five loaves of bread and two fish. Not only did the meager lunch become enough to feed thousands of people—it became more than enough! After everyone had eaten, there were still twelve baskets full of bread and fish left over! But before the small lunch became a mighty feast, before the little became much, before the miracle of multiplication could take place, it says in verse 19 that Jesus "took the five loaves and the two fish, and looking up toward heaven, He blessed the food, and breaking the loaves He gave them to the disciples, and the disciples gave to the crowds" (NAS). Notice something very important here. It says Jesus did two things: first, He blessed the food, and second, He broke it.

Jesus blesses only what He breaks. God can multiply only what has been broken. Do you want God to take your little life and do something mighty with it? Do you want to be blessed and be a blessing to multitudes? Then you need to be broken.

Verse 20 is careful to specify that the baskets left over were made up of "broken pieces"—"They picked up what was left over of the broken pieces, twelve full baskets" (NAS). At the end of our lives, when all is said and done, and everything has been consumed, the only parts of our lives that will have lasting value are the broken pieces. The way the world looks at things is so different from the way God looks at them. The world values the lofty, powerful, proud, and big. God values a broken and a contrite heart, a heart that is humble and bowed low before the King.

In Isaiah 66:2 the Lord says, "'This is the one I esteem: he who is humble and contrite in spirit, and trembles at my word'" (NIV). The psalmist says in Psalm 51:17, "The sacrifices of God are a broken spirit; a broken and contrite heart, O God, you will not despise" (NIV).

Hebrews 11:21 speaks about the great patriarch Jacob at the end of his life and describes him by saying he "leaned on the top of his staff" (NIV). Why is this detail important? Why even mention it? It is worth mentioning because Jacob had been defined by an encounter with the Lord that left him with a limp. The Jacob who limped was not the same Jacob who stole his brother's birthright and defrauded his elderly father. The limping Jacob was a broken man. Jacob had struggled all his life to obtain God's blessing through deceit and manipulation. He had stolen the blessing from his brother, Esau. He had embezzled the blessing of his father, Isaac. But it was only after he had been broken before the Lord that the Bible says he received the *true* blessing, the blessing of the Lord (Gen. 32:29).

Most people would have seen Jacob's limp as a handicap, but Jacob knew better. His limp was a memento of his life-changing encounter with God, which had left him broken and leaning. The broken Jacob was the blessed Jacob. This was the Jacob who became a mighty patriarch and the father of a nation that bears his new name, Israel.

At the Last Supper Jesus took the bread of Communion and said, "Take, eat: this is my body, which is broken for you" (1 Cor. 11:24). This brokenness that He spoke of was the crucifixion He would soon endure. That brokenness would loose the greatest power the world has ever known. The apostle Paul says, "I am crucified with Christ: nevertheless I live; yet not I, but Christ liveth in me" (Gal. 2:20). When we are crucified with Christ, this death to self is a brokenness that allows the life of Christ to flow out of us. A broken person is a person who is crucified with Christ. It is in this kind of person that God's will is being done and in whom God's kingdom is present and flowing out to the world around him.

Death to Your Vision

When we talk about being crucified with Christ and dying to self, what do we mean? It means we die to our desires, our ego, and our will. Sometimes this even means dying to our own vision. But you may say, "I'm sure my vision is God-given. It is His will." Yet there is an inherent danger. It is possible for the calling, promises, and vision God has given us to become our main ambition, making them opponents of God, for He is not willing to share our hearts with anything—not even with good things.

Isaac was the fulfillment of the promise God gave Abraham. Yet God was not willing to share Abraham's heart, not even with Isaac. So God asked Abraham to lay Isaac on the altar and offer him as a sacrifice, knowing this would be the ultimate test of Abraham's love. Author A. W. Tozer expounds on this brilliantly in his classic book *The Pursuit of God.*

> God let the suffering old man go through with it up to the point where He knew there would be no retreat, and then forbade him to lay a hand upon the boy. To the wondering patriarch He now says in effect, "It's all right, Abraham. I never intended that you should actually slay the lad. I only wanted to remove him from the temple of your heart that I might reign unchallenged there. I wanted to correct the perversion that existed in your love. Now you may have the boy, sound and well. Take him and go back to your tent. Now I know that thou fearest God, seeing that thou hast not withheld thy son, thine only son, from me."[1]

What does it mean to surrender our will to God? The word *surrender* is a radical word! Many of us are willing to surrender until it begins to hurt, but true surrender is painful. Some people are willing to surrender as long as it is logical, but true surrender is not subject to our rationale. Others can surrender what is bad and harmful, but God is not satisfied. To God surrender is not complete until it is all encompassing, exhaustive, total. It is not simply saying, "Your will be done," but it includes, "Not my will." This death to self is not some form of divine sadism. God always has life in mind. Just as a gardener prunes off the old branches so new ones can grow, God desires to remove that which hinders life and growth. This place of death is also the place of birth, and it is how God's purposes are born in the earth!

John Wimber is best known as the founder of the Vineyard church movement, which is well known for its wonderful music that touched the world and, in many ways, revolutionized worship in the modern church. But many people don't realize that John Wimber had been very successful as a secular musician. Two of his hit singles reached the US top ten before he met the Lord and abandoned fame and fortune to follow Jesus. His wife, Carol, told the following story:

> John and I had been Christians only a few months. We were broke and Christmas was coming. John had laid down his musical career because Jesus asked him to. After refusing a lucrative offer to arrange a Christmas album, he quietly put down the phone. As I watched, John went to the cupboards, closets and the piano bench. He gathered a lifetime of work and talent and placed it in big cardboard boxes and we drove to the Yorba Linda dump. As he pushed the last box out of the station wagon and it sunk into the garbage, John 12:24 came to my mind: "Except a grain of wheat fall into the earth and dies, it remains alone, but if it dies, it bears much fruit." In my heart I know that was when worship was born in the Vineyard.[2]

What if God asked you to give up the thing you enjoy the most? What if He asked you to lay down your gift or talent, the thing that defines you—the thing in which you find self-worth? Could you lay your promise on the altar as Abraham did Isaac, or push your treasures into the Dumpster as John Wimber did? Have you checked to see who is sitting on the throne of your heart? Is it you? Is it your vision? Is it your dream? Or is it Jesus?

My friend, God has a wonderful plan for your life, and He wants to use you in extraordinary ways for His glory. But resurrection only follows death—death to self, death to your will, death to your desires, and death to your dreams. It is in these painful moments of surrender that God's kingdom is established in us, when we pray with Jesus, "Not my will, but Yours be done." This beautiful broken-ness allows us to become an extension of God's dominion, and our lives become "cracks in the wall" through which His kingdom can come and His will can be done *in* earth and *on* earth!

Chapter 8

SECRET #3—HEARING GOD'S VOICE

W HEN I ATTENDED Southeastern University in Lakeland, Florida, the president of the university was Mark Rutland, PhD. I remember once hearing him tell a story about a time when he was flying out of Los Angeles after an intense time of ministry. He was tired and feeling rather unspiritual at that particular moment, but the man sitting next to him wanted to make conversation. "What do you do for a living?" this gentleman asked, to which Dr. Rutland replied, "I'm a Bible college president and a minister." The gentleman, who was also a minister, automatically assumed they were part of the same denomination. He continued to probe inquisitively until he discovered that Dr. Rutland was, in fact, affiliated with a Pentecostal denomination.

It was then that the gentleman realized they held very different doctrinal positions, and his demeanor immediately changed. His tone became argumentative, and he decided to take advantage of the opportunity to debate a real-live Pentecostal. "I have something I want to ask you," he said. Dr. Rutland was not in the mood for a debate. "Friend, can't we just relax and drink our Diet Coke?" he asked. But the man was insistent. "No," he said, "there is something I need to know. Please just answer this question: Since the canon of Scripture is closed, do you believe God still speaks? Because we don't."

Dr. Rutland reluctantly responded, still not wanting to engage in a debate. "OK," he said, "I'll answer your question if you'll answer mine: Are you or are you not called to preach?"

"Yes, of course, I'm called to preach," the man shot back.

"Then let me ask you," Dr. Rutland said, "who called you?" The gentleman had no reply. He turned his face to the window and never spoke to Dr. Rutland again for the rest of the trip.

Hearing the voice of God is one of the most basic and most profound secrets to discovering God's will for your life. In fact, without the ability to hear God's voice, knowing His will would actually be impossible. God speaks to people through a myriad of different means and methods, but many simply don't realize it. My friend, whether you know it or not, God is speaking to you, and your ability to recognize His voice is not only the key to discovering His will, but it is also the key to staying in His will for the rest of your life. Hearing the voice of God is not only possible for the child of God; it is absolutely imperative to listen to and be led by that voice!

Evangelist Reinhard Bonnke said, "It would be hard to find a line of Scripture on which to build a doctrine of a silent God. It is not at all the Bible picture. People called on God because that is how they knew Him—a God who can be heard. A silent heaven is frightening: 'If you remain silent, I will be like those who have gone down to the pit,' the Psalmist cried (Psalm 28:1)....In 1 Corinthians, Paul also contrasts 'dumb idols' (1 Corinthians 12:2) with the vocal gifts of the Spirit, tongues, prophecy, and interpretation, the word of knowledge and the word of wisdom. These utterances are God's gifts, typical of God who speaks."[1]

> Without the ability to hear God's voice, knowing His will would actually be impossible.

Jesus said, "But he who enters by the door is the shepherd of the sheep. To him the doorkeeper opens, and the sheep hear his voice; and he calls his own sheep by name and leads them out. And when he brings out his own sheep, he goes before them; and the sheep follow him, for they know his voice. Yet they will by no means follow a stranger, but will flee from him, for they do not know the voice of strangers" (John 10:2–5, NKJV). If we are a part of His flock, we have all been called by the voice of the Good Shepherd, and the voice that called us to salvation is the same voice that must lead us throughout our lives.

Honoring His Written Word

Any advice on hearing God's voice must invariably begin with what God has already revealed in Scripture. I am not saying this because I feel some religious duty to preface my "real" advice with a courtesy nod to the Bible. I can truly say that, for me personally, the most common way I have heard God's voice and sensed God's leading in my life is through the Scriptures. In fact, most of what is written in this book has come from what God has shown me as I have meditated on His Word.

The Scriptures are always speaking to anyone who will take the time to meditate on them. If you say you desire to hear God's voice yet have no desire to read the Bible, you are fooling yourself. The Scriptures ring with the pitch, the tone, the rhythm, and the meter of God's voice. You will learn to recognize His voice as you cultivate a deep, abiding love for what God has already said in His written Word. God has gone to great lengths to preserve His Word. Many righteous men and women have paid a dear price, even with their blood, so that we could have the Scriptures. If you are not interested enough in what God has already said to take the time to read His Word, then why should He say anything else to you?

I sent an e-mail to one of my staff members recently with detailed instructions on something that needed to be done. He came back to me right away asking for clarification. It was obvious to me that he had not taken the time to read my e-mail carefully because in it I had already answered all of his questions. Why should I repeat all of my instructions just because he didn't take the time to read what I had already said? I replied to his questions by simply resending my original e-mail. I think many times we are wondering why God doesn't speak to us, but it is so simple: He has already spoken, and we have not taken the time to read what He has said. The answers to many of our questions have been sitting right there in front of us all along gathering dust while we cry out to God for a word from heaven.

If the enemy can keep you from God's Word, he can keep you from God's voice. If you really want to hear the voice of God speaking, make time every day to meditate upon the Scriptures. Jesus said, "The words that I speak unto you, they are spirit, and they are life" (John 6:63). There is a dimension of supernatural awareness and sensitivity that seems to move to a heightened state in our lives when we simply spend time reading and meditating upon the Word of God. If we learn and know the sound of heaven by reading His Word, we are better able to recognize His voice when He speaks to us personally.

God Speaks Through the Holy Spirit

In the church many sincere, born-again believers have divided themselves into two camps. There are the "Spirit" people and the "Word" people. The "Spirit" people put their emphasis on the experiential aspects of Christianity: power, anointing, supernatural manifestations, and so on. The "Word" people prefer a more cerebral approach. They think of themselves as serious students of the Word and shy away from anything that seems to be emotionally driven. To me these distinctions are nonsense.

If any form of emotional and experiential Christianity is not based on Scripture, it is nothing more than New Age mysticism.

And if any form of Christianity is entirely cerebral and has no impact on real Word experience, it is nothing more than an empty shell. People of the Word must also be people of the Spirit, and people of the Spirit must also be people of the Word. There is no need to separate the two. In fact, to do so is dangerous!

In Ephesians 6 Paul talks about the "armor of God," which includes the belt of truth, the breastplate of righteousness, the shoes of the gospel of peace, the shield of faith, the helmet of salvation, and the sword of the Spirit, which is the Word of God (vv. 14–17). I want you to notice that we have no offensive weapon in this list. Now you will invariably disagree and point to the sword, the Word

> If you really want to hear the voice of God speaking, make time every day to meditate upon the Scriptures.

of God, but look carefully. The Word of God is not called "the sword of the Christian." It is called the sword of the Spirit. In other words, it belongs to the Spirit.

He alone can wield it properly. Without the illumination that the Holy Spirit brings, the Bible is just black ink on white paper. This is why some of the most disciplined students of Scripture, even professors and scholars, can be atheists and agnostics. These are people who are studying the Scriptures from a purely intellectual and cognitive perspective. These people have used the Bible to commit the sin of idolatry. All they see are objections, and all they gain is doubt. "The letter kills," Paul says, "but the Spirit gives life" (2 Cor. 3:6, NKJV).

At the end of Jesus's earthly ministry as He was preparing to die on the cross, He told His disciples, "But the Helper, the Holy Spirit, whom the Father will send in My name, He will teach you all things, and bring to your remembrance all things that I said to you" (John 14:26, NKJV). The Holy Spirit is not a doctrine or denomination or optional experience reserved for only a few Christians.

The importance of this truth cannot be overstated. He is the third person of the Trinity given by the Father in response to the prayer of Jesus to be and to do everything Jesus would do in our lives were He still here physically. Hearing the voice of God is actually hearing the voice of the Holy Spirit in our hearts. Without His active participation in our lives the heavens would be silent, for He is the one who reveals the voice of God in our hearts.

The more we give the Holy Spirit's presence a place of honor in our lives, the more sensitive we become to His voice. It's this fellowship and communion with the Holy Spirit that sharpens our spiritual sensitivity and makes our hearts better able to hear the voice of the Lord when He speaks to us.

Hearing His Voice Begins With "Turning Aside"

There is a small shrub called *dictamnus albus* that grows in Israel (as well as many other places). It is also known as the "gas plant" or "burning bush," because it emits a flammable vapor and has been said to spontaneously combust if it gets hot enough in the desert sun. Some Bible commentators believe the *dictamnus albus* might be the very species of bush Moses encountered.[2]

> And the angel of the LORD appeared unto him in a flame of fire out of the midst of a bush: and he looked, and, behold, the bush burned with fire, and the bush was not consumed. And Moses said, I will now turn aside, and see this great sight, why the bush is not burnt. And when the LORD saw that he turned aside to see, God called unto him out of the midst of the bush, and said, Moses, Moses. And he said, Here am I.
>
> —EXODUS 3:2–4

This is where Moses received his divine call and discovered God's will for his life. But there is an interesting detail recorded here that many people miss. First of all, it's important to note that

Moses was not impressed because a bush was on fire. He had lived in the wilderness for forty years. I'm sure he had encountered many *dictamnus albus* bushes before, and perhaps he had even seen them spontaneously combust. But this one was unique because it kept burning and burning and burning, and yet, "The bush was not consumed."

I don't know how long the bush burned before Moses realized something extraordinary was going on. Maybe it burned for a day or a week or a month before he decided to investigate the phenomenon. The Scriptures don't tell us. But one thing is certain. God never shouted out to Moses from the bush, "Hey, you—Moses! Come over here. I have something I want to say to you!" Instead God waited until verse 4. It says when the Lord saw that Moses turned aside to see, then and only then did God call out to him from the midst of the bush.

I have often been asked, "Why doesn't God speak to me?" I think many times the reason is so simple—we aren't listening! We are often so busy and in such a hurry that we rush right past the Lord and never stop to give Him our attention. I wonder how often we miss an encounter with God or a word from heaven simply because we are too busy to take the time to "turn aside." I have met some Christians who feel very sorry for themselves because it seems they are always being forgotten and passed over. While others have burning bush experiences and receive great revelations from God, they seem to always be left out. They ask, "Is God angry with me? Doesn't He love me? Aren't I special to Him?" My friend, perhaps God has just been waiting for you to slow down and "turn aside."

Several years ago I ministered in a church where a powerful move of the Holy Spirit caused tremendous growth because people were being saved and discipled. After one of the powerful services I saw a new convert talking to a deacon of the church. I was curious to know what they could be discussing, so I moved closer to listen. I heard the young man saying, "I've only been saved for a short time, and I struggle with prayer." The deacon said, "Young man, prayer is easy. It's just talking to God. Talk to Him like you would talk to a friend."

"Yes, I do that," the young man said, "but after about five minutes I've said everything I know to say. Yet I hear other people saying they pray for hours. How can someone pray for so long? What do they talk about?" The deacon began to explain. "First," he said, "you need to make a list of all your friends and relatives on a piece of paper. Then you need to list everything you need from God. Then you need to list everything you can be thankful for…" And the catalog of things to talk with God about went on and on. After the deacon finished giving his advice, I pulled the young man aside and said, "Do you really want to know the secret to prayer?"

"Yes" he said, "please tell me."

I said, "I can give it to you in one word: *listen.*"

My friend, as sincere as that deacon was, his advice to the young convert was terrible. If that young man had done what he was told to do, I'm sure his prayer life would have been exhausted within a week. Prayer is not about making lengthy lists of requests for God and continually chattering for as long as possible. Sometimes the best thing you can do is to *be quiet and listen!* When I am in the presence of someone who is full of wisdom and who has many years of rich life experience, I make it a point to keep my mouth shut and listen to what he has to say, because I know that what he has to say is more important than what I have to say.

Do you think for one second that what you have to say is more important than what God has to say? François Fénelon said, "A humility that is still talkative doesn't run very deep."[3] Learn to become quiet in the presence of the Lord, in a posture of humility and awe, and tune your spiritual ears to His voice. God will speak to you in this place, and you will encounter His presence as Moses did—when you turn aside and listen.

Discerning the Voice of the Lord

So you think God has spoken to you, but you're not completely sure? We've all been there. The truth is that sometimes God's voice is easy to recognize, and sometimes it's not. If there is a question in your mind about whether or not something you're sensing is from God, ask yourself the following questions.

Is it biblical?

If the answer to this question is no, then you have your answer. God will *never* tell you to do *anything* that is contrary to His Word. Even if what you are sensing feels so real and so strong, watch out! There are many spirits in the world but only one Holy Spirit. And the Holy Spirit will never contradict the Scriptures.

Is this causing confusion in my heart?

If the answer to this question is yes, then what you are sensing probably is not from God because God is not the author of confusion (1 Cor. 14:33). Jesus likened His people to sheep, and sheep are very easily frightened and confused. God may challenge us to think differently about things or to reach out to new levels of faith, but He doesn't create confusion or the doubt and strife that often accompany it.

Is this producing peace in my heart?

Jesus's voice comes with an awareness of heavenly peace. In contrast, the devil uses urgency, pressure, and fear to drive people. There can certainly be exceptions to this rule. Sometimes the Lord speaks words of correction and rebuke. There are also situations when the word of the Lord is time sensitive and immediate action is required. But most of the time when God speaks, it is not a driving, demanding, high-pressure, "You have to do this *right now* or else!"

word. If you believe God is speaking to warn you of imminent danger and you must react quickly, then do so. But if you believe God is speaking to you to quit your job, sell your house, and go to the mission field before next Thursday, it might be best to slow down a bit, get into the Word, and seek some godly counsel.

Have I quieted my desires and self-interest?

The voice of our own longings, interests, and opinions can easily be confused with God's voice. To make sure what we are hearing is from God, we must identify our desires and self-interests and, as an intentional act of our will, neutralize them. The louder the voice of our own will, the quieter God's voice will be. Conversely, the quieter the voice of our own will, the louder God's voice will be. Therefore, if what you are sensing grows quieter as you silence your desires, then it is not from God. But if what you are sensing grows stronger as you neutralize your own desires, then it just might be from the Holy Spirit.

Become Familiar With His Voice

Have you ever been in a crowded place such as a shopping mall at Christmastime and heard the sound of someone you love calling out your name? Despite all the noise, Christmas music, and multitudes of busy shoppers, you recognized that familiar sound above everything else because it was someone you love.

God seldom speaks to strangers who have no time for Him, and even if He did, they would not recognize His voice. He loves to speak to people who love Him and desire to live their lives in His presence. He draws near to those who, as an act of their will, have drawn near to Him (James 4:8). The more time we spend alone with Him seeking His face through prayer and worship, the easier it becomes to hear and immediately recognize His voice in our hearts. The greater our love for Him, the more finely tuned our ears will become to hear the sound of His voice.

God does speak to His people by His Spirit. The challenge is in learning to hear and then having the determination, faith, and love to simply obey what He is saying. We can all hear the voice of God if we will learn to listen. "For as many as are led by the Spirit of God, they are the sons of God" (Rom. 8:14).

Chapter 9

SECRET #4—THE WAY UP IS DOWN

IN THE SEVENTIES and eighties CBS broadcast a hit sitcom called *The Jeffersons.* The show featured an African American family who became wealthy and moved out of a run-down area in Queens to a luxury apartment in Manhattan. As they celebrated their new-found promotion, the Jeffersons used to talk about "movin' on up," a phrase that has since become synonymous with the sitcom.

Whenever we speak of advancement or promotion, we tend to think of it as upward motion—climbing the ladder, breaking the glass ceiling, getting on top of the heap, upgrading, elevating, etc.—but nothing says it better than "movin' on up."

Up. It is the direction everyone wants to go, for the path upward seems to be the path to fame, fortune, honor, and glory. But isn't it interesting that many of earth's most precious substances can be acquired only by digging deep down? The person who is willing to go very low could become very wealthy. Engineers also understand that if they want to raise a tall building, first they need to go low and lay a deep foundation. So it is with promotion. Jesus said, "He who humbles himself will be exalted" (Luke 14:11, NKJV). The low path of humility is the only way to promotion with God.

Joseph had lofty dreams of greatness. He saw his mother, father, and brothers all bowing down before him. But God's way of promoting Joseph to the top was not what he would have imagined. Ironically, it was those very dreams of glory that bred contempt in the hearts of his brothers, who eventually sold him into a humble life of slavery.

Joseph's path to greatness would take him through the lowlands of servitude, character assassination, and even imprisonment in the royal dungeon. For a while Joseph's life seemed to have a downward trajectory, constantly going from bad to worse. I'm sure there were moments when he must have asked, "Why, God?" Wasn't it God who had promised him promotion and influence? Had Joseph done something wrong? Is that why God was allowing him to go through such hardship?

Joseph descended the dark, winding staircase of humility and submission. When he reached the last door at the bottom, he discovered that this obscure, downward path had led him all the way to...the top! Almost overnight he found himself in one of the

> God's will for your life always leads you on the path of humility.

highest places of power and authority in the world. All along it was this lowly path that God had determined to use to lift Joseph up. Joseph discovered that *the way up is down*.

Perhaps the greatest example of this principle comes from Jesus Christ Himself. He who was "in the form of God, thought it not robbery to be equal with God: but made himself of no reputation, and took upon him the form of a servant, and was made in the likeness of men: and being found in fashion as a man, he humbled himself, and became obedient unto death, even the death of the cross. Wherefore God also hath highly exalted him, and given him a name which is above every name: that at the name of Jesus every knee should bow, of things in heaven, and things in earth, and things under the earth;

and that every tongue should confess that Jesus Christ is Lord, to the glory of God the Father" (Phil. 2:6–11).

The world teaches us that we live in a dog-eat-dog world, and if we want to advance we need to fight for our rights, prove ourselves, and step on the competition if necessary. But Psalm 75:6–7 tells us that "promotion cometh neither from the east, nor from the west, nor from the south. But God is the judge: he putteth down one, and setteth up another." If we want to be promoted, it would be wise to heed the advice of the one who gives promotions:

- "For whoever exalts himself will be humbled, and he who humbles himself will be exalted" (Luke 14:11, NKJV).

- "Blessed are the meek, for they shall inherit the earth" (Matt. 5:5, NKJV).

- "Humble yourselves in the sight of the Lord, and He will lift you up" (James 4:10, NKJV).

- "A man's pride [arrogance] will bring him low, but the humble in spirit will retain honor" (Prov. 29:23, NKJV).

- "For not he who commends himself is approved, but whom the Lord commends" (2 Cor. 10:18, NKJV).

The Way Up Is Down
Scan QR code

or visit
LiveBeforeYouDieBook.com/3

The first time I ever visited the Eiffel Tower, I noticed that there were three different queues you could join. One went to the first level, one went to the second level, and one went all the way to the top. To come all the way to Paris and go only to the first or second level seemed ridiculous. I was determined to go to the top. I could see how the first- and second-level queues were climbing the stairs going immediately up, but for some strange reason my queue was headed downward. It seemed strange for the queue going the highest to be moving downward, but soon I saw the reason. While the other queues were climbing the stairs with their hands and feet, we were making our way to a lift that would take us all the way to the top.

God's will for your life always leads you on the path of humility. Don't make the mistake of thinking the humble path is the way for losers. Some people are so eager to be successful that they are climbing level by level with all their might, proving themselves and promoting themselves with feverish urgency. But you should know that God has an elevator waiting for those who want to go higher than level one or level two. And the only way to get to God's lift is to go down to the low place of humility and submission. This is the path Jesus walked, and it leads to the loftiest place in existence. The way up is down.

Chapter 10

SECRET #5—TAKE ACTION!

A CERTAIN WELL-KNOWN EVANGELIST was attending a convention in Indianapolis about mass evangelism. Inspired by the stirring messages he was hearing about winning the lost, he went with his song leader to the street corner during an intermission that evening. The song leader stood on a box and began to sing. When a crowd had gathered, the evangelist began to preach. Soon so many people had assembled that the throng was spilling into the streets. The evangelist thought it best to invite the people to follow him to the nearby convention hall where the evangelism conference was being held. Soon the auditorium was filled with spiritually hungry people, and the evangelist began to preach the gospel to them passionately.

After a while the convention delegates returned from their dinner break to find street people now occupying some of their reserved seats. The delegates began to mutter and complain amongst themselves. The nerve of this evangelist to impose himself this way—*who does he think he is?* The convention leaders deliberated about what should be done and then sent a representative to the evangelist to tell him their verdict. The evangelist was in mid-sermon when the messenger approached and whispered into his ear. The evangelist stopped preaching and said to the crowd who had come to hear the gospel, "Now we must close, as the brethren of the convention wish to come and discuss the topic 'How to Reach the Masses.'"

There always seems to be a great divide in life between action and intention, between works and words, between doing something and merely talking about doing it. And it is in this space, between desire and deed, where most people die in a wilderness of inaction. For every go-getter who is ready to take the field, there are a thousand professional conference delegates who are content to go on endlessly discussing the need without ever actually doing anything. But the ones who will go on to see God's will fulfilled in their lives are people of action, initiative, and urgency.

In the Christian world many people spend their whole lives waiting for God to do something for them. They talk about waiting for God's timing or provision; they are looking for God to "make a way," "open doors," and give "divine appointments." Although there will certainly be situations in life when we need to wait for the Lord, many times (perhaps even most times, if we are honest) the real underlying reason for our inaction is far less spiritual than we would like to believe. In the secular world people have the same hangup, except instead of "waiting for God" they are waiting for "the right moment" or "the perfect opportunity." For saint and sinner alike these perfect moments almost never come.

> The ones who will go on to see God's will fulfilled in their lives are people of action, initiative, and urgency.

I was talking with a young woman recently who wants to attend a certain Bible college. With whimsical indifference she told me she wasn't sure when she would go. She said there were quite a number of obstacles in her way (mostly financial), and she believed that if it was really God's will, He would "prepare the way" for her. In other words, she thought that if she was really supposed to attend this Bible college, God would solve all of her problems, pay all of her bills, and roll out a red carpet for her. This kind of thinking makes me want to stand on a table and scream!

Where is the urgency? Where is the passion? Where is the chutzpah? If you want God to part the sea for you, but you are not even willing to get your toes wet, you are living in a fantasy world—this is simply not the way it works. Even when God is fully in something and has ordained it, He rarely arranges all the aspects of our lives so that everything is perfect and easy. On the contrary, in many cases God's will for your life will seem like the more difficult path, and it will have to be pursued with real determination. Jesus said, "The kingdom of heaven suffereth violence, and the violent take it by force" (Matt. 11:12). God is looking for the burning-hearted, not the faint-hearted.

One of my favorite scriptures is Daniel 11:32, "But the people who know their God shall stand firm and take action" (ESV). Anyone who knows God and understands His ways will know that God expects us to take action. God cannot bless our good intentions, only what we actually do!

Jesus told a parable in Matthew 21:28–31. "There was a man who had two sons. He went to the first and said, 'Son, go and work today in the vineyard.' 'I will not,' he answered, but later he changed his mind and went. Then the father went to the other son and said the same thing. He answered, 'I will, sir,' but he did not go. Which of the two did what his father wanted? 'The first,' they answered" (NIV).

The moral of the story is clear: good intentions and empty promises are not enough. God is looking for men and women of action! "Be ye doers of the word," James says, "and not hearers only" (James 1:22).

Second Corinthians 9:10 says God gives seed to the sower. God's way is counter-intuitive. We would say, "God should first provide the seed, then I will sow." But God says, "Sow first, and then I will provide the seed." While we are waiting for God to provide, God is waiting for us to act. It is our demonstrated faith that moves God's heart and hand, not just our need.

Get Moving

In order to fly, an airplane needs "lift." Lift comes from speed, and speed comes from "thrust." Thrust is the power that pushes the aircraft forward, and without it nothing else matters. The aerodynamic design, the well-trained pilot in the cockpit, the sophisticated navigational technology, and the tank full of jet fuel are all useless unless the engines come alive and provide forward motion. In your life the only one who can provide the forward motion is you. God will be your pilot. He will provide the wind beneath your wings and the fuel in your tank, but you have to give Him some momentum to work with. You cannot do God's part, and God will not do your part. Your part is to get into gear, get off your backside, and get moving. Reinhard Bonnke has said, "God will lift you out of the deepest pit, but He won't lift you out of an easy chair—you have to do that yourself." So what are you waiting for? How long will you do nothing while you grow old in the wilderness of inaction?

It is true that God opens doors, and sometimes particular doors are not opened for a variety of reasons. But it is very unlikely that *all* the doors are shut. Imagine a man sitting at a red light in the downtown area of a big city. The light in front of him turns green, but when he looks ahead he sees that the next five lights are still red. Should he sit at the green light in front of him and just wait for all the other lights to turn green as well? Of course not! He should move through the green light he has. Yet many people fail to move through the green light God has given them because they foresee obstacles ahead that they don't know how to handle.

In Joshua 3 we read about the children of Israel encountering the obstacle of the Jordan River, which was overflowing and impossible to cross. In obedience to the Lord Joshua told the priests to take the ark of the covenant and go forward into the waters of the Jordan.

This surely would have seemed like a ridiculous idea, but look at what happened.

> And when those who carried the ark came into the Jordan, and the feet of the priests carrying the ark were dipped in the edge of the water...the waters which were flowing down from above stood and rose up in one heap....So the people crossed opposite Jericho.
>
> —JOSHUA 3:15–16, NAS

Now if Joshua had been trained in one of our fine Bible colleges, he probably would have given more mature advice. He would have said, "Gentlemen, we are going to wait right here until the Lord 'opens a door' for us." But if that had been his command, their skeletons would still be decomposing somewhere on the banks of the Jordan River, because the water was not going to part for them until their feet got wet! My friend, sometimes you need to just go ahead and get your feet wet in faith and see what the Lord will do for you!

In Matthew 14:22–29 we read the story of how Peter walked on the water. It was early in the morning when Jesus came walking toward the disciples' boat on the turbulent sea. When the disciples saw Him, they thought it was a ghost and

> God cannot bless our good intentions, only what we actually do!

they cried out in fear, but Jesus said, "Take courage! It is I. Don't be afraid."

"Lord, if it's You," Peter replied, "tell me to come to You on the water."

"Come," He said.

Notice that Jesus didn't say, "Peter, come." He simply said, "Come." Do you realize what this means? Any of the disciples could have responded to that word and walked on the water. People often criticize Peter for taking his eyes off Jesus and sinking, but I admire him for being the only one willing to get out of the boat. You will never walk on water if you're not willing to step out of the boat!

This secret is so simple and yet underemphasized in the Christian world. Some people seem to think that taking action demonstrates a lack of faith. On the contrary, faith *without* works is dead! Said another way, *faith without action is dead!* All of the planning, waiting, and wishing is wasted time if you are not going to take action. If you want to learn to swim, you are going to have to go ahead and take the plunge.

We are usually all too aware of our inadequacies and deficiencies. The best way to address these issues is to begin to move forward. Momentum and motion will make everything in your life easier to steer. As you move forward, you'll discover what really needs your attention, you'll be incentivized to deal with it urgently, you'll make the needed adjustments, and you'll be able to empirically gauge your progress. You'll discover that many of your previous concerns were nonsense and that you had never even considered many of the real issues you needed to confront.

Jack Canfield, the very successful businessman and author, wrote about this secret in his best-selling book *The Success Principles*: "Successful people have a bias for action. Most successful people I know have a low tolerance for excessive planning and talking about it. They are antsy to get going. They want to get started. They want the games to begin...Planning has its place, but it must be kept in perspective. Some people spend their whole lives waiting for the perfect time to do something. There's rarely a 'perfect' time to do anything. What is important is to just get started. Get into the game. Get on the playing field. Once you do, you will start to get feedback that will help you make the corrections you need to make to be successful."[1]

Ready, Fire, Aim

The other day I went with my father to the shooting range. He was heading out on a hunting trip, and before he left I wanted to help him "sight in" the rifle I had bought him as a gift. We looked through the scope, which we had just attached, aimed at the target, and fired, knowing that we would most likely miss the bull's-eye. But by firing at the target, we could see where we needed to make an adjustment to the scope. We were only able to make corrections when we saw how we were missing the mark. I think this is typical of life. We usually learn more from our mistakes than our successes. But unless you fire, you will never miss, and unless you miss, you will never be able to make the adjustments necessary to hit the bull's-eye.

Whenever I begin a new project or initiative, I never view my initial plan as the final draft. I dive into it knowing that I will learn as I go. This means that I'm not paralyzed by a fear of failure; rather I am looking forward to learning what not to do. I see my initial plan as an uncalibrated machine with many dials. The dials are all the different variables represented in that particular project. Once the machine is running, I can see what is working and what is not working. I am diligent to gather sufficient feedback, and then I will begin to tweak the "dials" based on that feedback.

Even when I feel like everything is running smoothly, I will continue to step back often to analyze the process. If something is working well, I will try to capitalize on it. If something is not working well, I will adjust it or prune it off altogether. It is an ongoing dynamic development that never ends. This process is where real progress is made, but until you take action, all of your planning and strategizing is simply untested theory.

Having said all these things, let me be clear: taking action is not just a matter of trial and error. At its core, it is a matter of faithfulness. Even if there are a thousand things you cannot do for one reason or another, there is always something you can do. It may seem small or insignificant, but the eyes of God are on you. He is watching to see what you will do with the opportunities He has given you, and your response will determine whether He entrusts you with more.

I was preaching in a church some time ago when a young man came up to me with tears in his eyes and said, "I have a calling like yours. The Lord has called me to preach the gospel. I believe I am going to win millions of people to the Lord, but I don't know where to start." I put my arm around him and said, "I think I can help you." He said, "You can?" I said, "Yes, I can tell you where to start. Start by telling your unsaved family members about Jesus. Then go and tell your unsaved friends about Jesus. Then go out to the street corners and preach the gospel to lost people wherever you can find them. As God sees your faithfulness, He will give you more."

Another young man shared his vision with me one day. He said, "I am going to start a house of prayer. I am going to have prayer, intercession, and worship going on twenty-four hours per day, seven days per week, three hundred sixty-five days per year."

"That's a wonderful vision," I said. "When will it begin?" He said, "Well, first I need to gather several dozen worship bands together and several hundred intercessors who share my vision." I could see a problem in his plan right away. "Can I give you some advice?" I asked. He was very eager to hear it. I said, "Why don't you start with one evening per week or one day per month? Start by doing whatever you *can* do, and as you are faithful, God will give you more." Unfortunately my advice was too unexciting for that young man. He decided to do it the more dramatic way and wait until all the bands and intercessors had been assembled. I'm sad to report that several years later, he still has not started the house of prayer.

I did not start by preaching to millions of people. I started preaching as a teenager to lost people on the streets. I went door to door in my neighborhood and witnessed to my neighbors. I went to the parks and stood on park benches and preached. I stood up in restaurants, outside movie theaters, on street corners. I have been escorted away by police on more than one occasion for preaching the gospel. When I first launched into full-time evangelistic ministry, I had only one preaching invitation. But that invitation led to another and another and another. Today I have more invitations than I could ever accept, but it all happened one door at a time.

There's an ancient Chinese proverb that says, "The journey of a thousand miles begins with the first step." Perhaps you don't know how to get from A to Z, but you don't need to know that. All you need to know is how to get from A to B. Once you get to B, then you will go to C, and one step at a time you will find that the waters will begin to part as your feet get wet.

PART 3

FIVE ENEMIES OF GOD'S WILL FOR YOUR LIFE

Chapter 11

ENEMY #1—THE BANDIT OF LAZINESS

IT'S ONE THING to know God's will. It's something else to do it. Discovering God's will makes very little difference unless we are willing to move forward in obedience. Someone said, "Even if you are on the right track, you will get run over if you just sit there." Many people seeking God's will have been "overrun" by those actually doing it.

Doing the will of God requires taking action. I'm talking about something very down-to-earth right now. Not just inspiration but perspiration. Not just divine revelation but also human effort. There are many people who are ineffective and unfruitful, not because they are not anointed, gifted, or equipped but simply because they are lazy. The writer of Proverbs 24 says he went past the field of a lazy man. He saw how thorns and weeds had covered the ground and swallowed the walls, which were in ruins.

> I applied my heart to what I observed and learned a lesson from what I saw: a little sleep, a little slumber, a little folding of the hands to rest—and poverty will come on you like a bandit and scarcity like an armed man.
> —PROVERBS 24:32–34, NIV

This lazy man's field was in shambles. It looked as though bandits had stolen his crop and ruined his livelihood. But his real enemy was not thieves or robbers; it was his own lack of effort. Laziness is a bandit that robs us of our potential, and it is an enemy of God's best for our lives. Yet here's the problem—nobody thinks he is lazy. If I randomly approached people on the street and asked, "Are you a lazy person?", I'd guess nine out of ten would say, "No!"

Most people think they are hardworking. In fact, people constantly tell me how busy they are and how little time they have. Yet a person can be very busy and still be lazy if he is avoiding some critical action that needs to be taken. I use the term *critical action* because not all activity is created equal. In the last chapter we talked about the importance of taking action, but now I want to make a distinction between effective action and mere busyness. Critical action is the kind of activity that produces real results, cuts through all the fluff, and gets right down to what is vital. Let me define laziness then as choosing to evade or compromise critical action.

Evasive Action

Twenty percent of people identify themselves as chronic procrastinators.[1] Their procrastination impacts every area of their lives. They don't mail their bills on time. They don't file their tax returns on time. They wait until Christmas Eve to do their Christmas shopping. They wait until the last minute to complete school assignments. They miss many opportunities because they always delay taking critical action. In fact, their dawdling is so reliable some companies count on it for profitability, offering, for instance, generous rebates that will surely never be redeemed.

What's amazing is that these procrastinators do not always appear to be lazy people. In fact, they are often the busiest of all! However, though they are busy, they are not taking critical action. It's important to recognize this distinction. Not only is there a difference between busyness and critical action, but also I have found that a great deal of that busyness is actually time invested in inventing ways to evade critical action. For this reason the word *procrastination* (with its passive implications) seems like an oxymoron. Because procrastination is apparently quite a lot of work, I prefer to call it *evasive action*. There is a poem that describes this perfectly.

> I've gone for a drink and sharpened my pencils,
> Searched through my desk for forgotten utensils.
> I reset my watch, I adjusted my chair,
> I've loosened my tie and straightened my hair.
> I filled my pen and tested the blotter
> And gone for another drink of water
> Adjusted the calendar, and raised the blind
> And I've sorted erasers of all different kinds.
> Now down to work I can finally sit.
> Oops, too late, it's time to quit.[2]

I encountered a book once that changed my life even though I never actually read it. In fact, I never even cracked open the cover, and I have no idea who wrote it. All I needed to see was the title: *Do It Now!* I once was a master of evasive action. I was very good at inventing reasons a certain critical action could not be taken at that moment. There were always a myriad of reasons more planning or strategizing was necessary before something could be done. But when I saw the title of that book, something amazing happened. I think the Holy Spirit must have used it to convict me because afterward when I was tempted to procrastinate, I started to hear that little phrase ringing in my ear, "Do it now!" It made a huge, positive difference in my life. I pray that from now on, you will also begin to hear those words ringing in your ears—"Do it now!" It will change your life as well!

The Compromise

To procrastinate is to evade critical action, but there is another way to avoid taking critical action that may be even more problematic. Let me call it the *comfortable compromise.* Comfortable compromise is difficult to define because, as with critical action, it will mean different things in different scenarios. Perhaps the best way to understand the distinction is by contrast.

While critical action is the most direct and effective action possible, placing the success of the mission ahead of personal well-being (security, comfort, and convenience), the comfortable compromise is a willingness to settle for a less effective action in the interest of self-preservation. Critical action almost always involves putting "boots on the ground," taking risks, and interacting with people in a way that makes one vulnerable.

Critical action will almost always mean paying some price and sticking your neck out in some way. The comfortable compromise, on the other hand, always consists of more talking than walking. It allows us to stay safe, makes us feel good about ourselves, and keeps us busy, but it produces very few actual results. Simply put, the comfortable compromise is an action that serves as a substitute for the critical action. It is a cheap imitation, a second-rate alternative, an easy way out.

I say that comfortable compromise is more problematic than procrastination because when we procrastinate, at least we know that something is still lacking. But the comfortable compromise allows us to pacify our conscience, feeling as though we have fulfilled our obligation though in reality we have accomplished only a fraction of our potential, or perhaps none at all.

Because I am an evangelist, the examples that come most readily to mind are those having to do with soul-winning. So please allow me to get on my soapbox for a moment. There is no more important or urgent matter in the universe than the salvation of the lost. It's no wonder Jesus's last words on earth were instructions to take the gospel to the ends of the world. This divine directive is commonly known as the Great Commission, and it is perhaps most clearly stated in Mark 16:15, "Go ye into all the world, and preach the gospel to every creature."

With so much at stake it is not surprising that Jesus's command here is extremely clear and direct. It contains two explicit critical actions: "go" and "preach." Had Jesus simply said, "Be sure to make a positive impact on the world," we would never have known exactly what action to take. But Jesus knew the salvation of the lost depended on two specific critical actions, "going" and "preaching."

> The comfortable compromise is an action that serves as a substitute for the critical action. It is a cheap imitation, a second-rate alternative, an easy way out.

I've heard it taught that the most effective way to win the lost is simply by living a good life, being kind to your neighbor, and "letting your light shine" wherever you are. While these are all good things, if they become a substitute for "going" and "preaching," they are nothing more than comfortable compromises. It amazes me the incredibly creative things people come up with to try to impact the world and society without having to go and preach the gospel. Churches and ministries spend enormous amounts of time, money, and energy every year on programs and activities through which they hope to reach the lost without taking the two critical actions Jesus commanded.

Yet for all the multiplied billions of dollars spent in American churches each year, attendance continues to fall, and very little fruit remains. Even in the high-tech, modern age in which we live, when it comes to the salvation of the lost, the critical actions remain the same as they were two thousand years ago when Jesus first commanded them. More effective actions will never be devised. The original ones, though foolish in their simplicity, will forever remain the most efficient and effective way to win the world—*go* and *preach the gospel*!

The Power of Urgency

The Bible is absolutely full of stories of men and women who succeeded when they took critical action and failed when they avoided it.

When David showed up on the battlefield where the Israelites were at a stalemate with the Philistines, he saw Goliath defying the armies of Israel and hurling insults at her God (1 Sam. 17). He knew immediately what action needed to be taken. He could have chosen to start a petition or lead a protest. He could have asked that a formal statement be issued from the government condemning Goliath's insensitivity toward the Israelites' religious beliefs. He might have even organized a prayer meeting to ask God to remove Goliath.

But as a shepherd boy David had faced a lion and a bear. He had learned the importance of critical action. He didn't have time to go home and exercise to build up his muscles in preparation for the great showdown. He didn't set up a target and start practicing with his slingshot. He simply took immediate, decisive, and critical action. While all the other Israelites stood on the battlefield procrastinating or looking for an easy way out, David had only one mission—to decapitate the giant. He did it, the deadlock was broken, and the battle was won that same day.

Saul, on the other hand, was always looking for a comfortable compromise. God told him to "go and utterly destroy the sinners the Amalekites, and fight against them until they are consumed" (1 Sam. 15:18). Saul almost obeyed. He conquered and destroyed the Amalekite city, but wholesale slaughter of the Amalekites seemed so extreme and so unnecessary. Surely he could achieve the same outcome with less brutality. So Saul decided to spare Agag, the king of the Amalekites, along with many of his people, sheep, and oxen, which Saul kept as spoils of war. Saul didn't realize that what God had prescribed was not merely a good suggestion; it was the critical action necessary to secure the kingdom. Saul's unwillingness to do what had to be done was irresponsible and disobedient. God decided to take the kingdom from Saul and give it to another—David.

Remember, we are talking about the *bandit of laziness*, and rather than defining laziness as doing nothing (because by that definition none of us think we are lazy), I am defining it as evading or compromising critical action (which we are all guilty of). The key then is to take critical action, but it is not always clear in every situation what the critical action is. To sort through the clutter, ask yourself, *Is there a more direct and effective way to do this?* If the answer is yes, then ask yourself, *Why am I choosing to avoid the more effective way?* If your honest self-examination reveals that you have simply chosen the path of least resistance, pleasure over pain, or what is most convenient for you personally, you may conclude that you have chosen the comfortable compromise. In other words, you are being lazy!

So how do we identify critical action? Because there are so many diverse situations, let me give a broad principle: *direct action is inspired by urgency.* Our perception of urgency not only compels us to take action but also prescribes what action is to be taken. For instance, if you saw someone about to fall off the edge of a cliff, you would not sit down to send him an e-mail about his precarious situation. You would immediately shout to him, run to him, reach to him, and so on.

> God will not honor laziness, and it will always keep you from fulfilling your calling.

If urgency compels and prescribes direct action, and direct action is the opposite of laziness, then the antidote for laziness is urgency. You need to see the importance of what you are doing. You need to realize there is much at stake. You need to remind yourself that the eyes of God are upon you. You need to stir yourself, shake yourself, and wake up.

A pastor once told me that he simply couldn't get new people to visit his church. I was convinced that his problem was a lack of urgency and action, so I asked him this question, "What if I told you I would give you a million dollars for every new person you could get to come to church next Sunday? Do you think you could figure out a way to do it?" He looked down and smiled. "Yes, for a million dollars I'm sure I could find a way," he said. If something can be done for a million dollars, then it can be done—period! If something *can* be done and *needs* to be done but is not being done, then the person responsible for doing it is neglecting his responsibility. Whether that neglect is the result of evasive action or comfortable compromise, it is a form of laziness.

Laziness is a thief that will rob you of God's best for your life. God will not honor laziness, and it will always keep you from fulfilling your calling. My friend, please let this point sink into your heart. Talent cannot substitute for action. Intelligence cannot substitute for action. Anointing, prayer, and fasting can't substitute for action. Even prophetic words cannot substitute for action. Fulfilling God's will for our lives is going to require putting off compromise, procrastination, and laziness. It is always going to require taking critical action—that means it's going to require diligence, discipline, risk, and good old-fashioned hard work!

Chapter 12

ENEMY #2—THE CEMETERY OF FEAR

IN MATTHEW 25 Jesus told a parable about a man who went on a journey to a faraway land. Before he left, he entrusted three servants with various "talents," or money. Rather than letting his money sit in a vault, the master decided to divide it among three servants so they could invest it and his fortune could increase while he was away. To the first servant the master gave five talents, to the second servant he gave two talents, and to the third servant he gave one talent.

The first two servants invested their money wisely, and it doubled in value. The third servant was concerned about the possibility of losing his talent, so he buried it in the ground. When the master returned, it was a time of reckoning. With the first two servants, the master was very pleased, but with the third servant who buried the one talent, the master was very angry. The master called him a wicked and lazy servant. He repossessed the one talent the servant had been given and had him cast

> Courage is *not* the absence of fear. In fact, there is no courage without fear. Courage is the willingness to face fear.

out into the darkness "where there will be weeping and gnashing of teeth" (Matt. 25:30, NIV).

I want you to notice the reason this servant gave for burying his talent. The servant said, "So I was afraid and went out and hid your talent in the ground" (Matt. 25:25, NIV). He buried his talent in the ground because of fear.

Fear causes many people to bury their talents in the ground. I'm not talking about the ground in your backyard. Genesis 2:7 says God formed man from the dust of the ground—*we* are the ground! People bury their talents within themselves because of fear—fear of failure, fear of being mocked, fear of hard work, fear of the unknown, spirits of fear, and fear of man, just to name a few.

I think one of the most tragic places you could ever visit is a cemetery, not because of the people who are buried there but because of what is buried within the people who are buried there: books and songs that were never written, sermons that were never preached, forgiveness that was never granted, inventions that were never developed—so much potential that was never realized. So much has been buried and lost for all eternity because someone was afraid of being hurt, afraid of criticism, afraid of rejection, afraid of financial difficulty or physical danger.

Evangelist Leonard Ravenhill said author and preacher A. W. Tozer once told him, "I'm not too worried about the judgment on my Christian life. It's the things I could have done but didn't do that worry me."[1] My friends, one day we are all going to stand before the Master and give an account of what He has entrusted to us. Oh, that we would fear that day above all and be willing to risk everything so on that day we would not be ashamed.

Notice that the servant was cast into outer darkness where there will be weeping and gnashing of teeth. Scholars disagree about whether or not this verse is referring to hell, but one thing is certain (and I think it is the main point), it is talking about deep regret, sorrow, and remorse over something that has been lost forever and can never be undone. Many people talk about the emotions they will feel when they arrive in heaven. There are popular songs about how we will dance and be overwhelmed with joy. But many will experience a very different emotion when they arrive in heaven—regret. In that moment all of their earthly fears will seem so impotent and distant, a hazy memory, like a dream that you can't quite remember. But the impact of those fears will be felt for eternity. It will be too late to go back and do what should have been done, and wave after wave of regret will wash over many people. No wonder Revelation 21:4 says Jesus will have to wipe the tears from their eyes.

Buried Talents
Scan QR code

or visit
LiveBeforeYouDieBook.com/4

When I was a teenager, I went on a missions trip to England and stayed in a "host home" with a lovely British couple. I'll never forget a poster they had hanging on their wall that reported the results of a survey given to ten groups of people. There was a group of ten-year-olds, twenty-year-olds, thirty-year-olds, all the way up to hundred-year-olds, and each was asked the same question: "What is your number one regret at this point in your life?" All the answers were interesting, some were funny, but the only answer I remember was from those who were a hundred years old. For some reason it is burned into my memory, and I can never forget it. After living a long life, they said their number one regret was that they "should have taken more risks." I determined then, as a very young man, that when I come to the end of my life I don't want to look back and realize that I never really lived at all because I was too afraid.

To many people fear seems to be a legitimate reason not to do something. But I want you to see that the master in Jesus's parable was not sympathetic toward the servant who buried his talent. When the servant said, "I was afraid," the master did not put his arm around him and say, "There, there, it's all right. You poor little servant. I'm sorry I put you in such an uncomfortable position." No, the master rebuked him sharply with anger and said, "You lazy servant!"

Why did the master accuse the servant of laziness? Because rather than facing his fears and taking a risk for his master's sake, he chose to take the easy path: bury the talent, stay at home, and relax. If you think fear is a good excuse for not doing God's will, you'd better think again. If you want to know how to overcome your fears, there is only one way—face them! Most of the time fear is like a mirage; as you walk toward it, it will become more and more transparent until it disappears completely. But to face your fears requires courage.

After Moses died, his protégé, Joshua, became the new leader. God promised to be with Joshua as He had been with Moses. God promised to give Joshua every place upon which the sole of his foot would tread. God promised to prosper Joshua wherever he went. But there was one requirement: "Only be strong and very courageous," the Lord said (Josh. 1:7, NKJV). Imagine you are about to embark on the most challenging undertaking of your life. You have no idea what lies before you, and then the Lord comes to you and says, "Be very courageous." That would scare me! Why? Because courage is

> Our talent does not belong to us—it belongs to the Master. He has entrusted it into our hands. But one day He will return, and we will have to give an account for what we did with His investment.

only needed in the presence of danger. Courage is *not* the absence of fear. In fact, there is no courage without fear. Courage is the willingness to face fear. All the promises, victories, and destiny awaiting Joshua were dependent on his willingness to face his fear.

If fulfilling God's will for our lives were just a matter of promoting our own names, reputations, and personal destinies, I would say, "Don't even bother. Stay home, watch television, and enjoy a comfortable, quiet life." But we must remember that what is at stake is God's eternal kingdom! Our talent does not belong to us—it belongs to the master. He has entrusted it into our hands. But one day He will return, and we will have to give an account for what we did with His investment.

Chapter 13

ENEMY #3—THE POISON OF UNBELIEF

A S WE DISCUSSED earlier, one of the characteristics of God's will is that God calls us to do the impossible! But to face the impossible requires faith. Satan knows that if he can inject unbelief into our spirits, he can effectively rob us of God's best for our lives. For this reason unbelief is a deadly enemy of God's plan for your life.

I think many of God's people don't realize how sinister and dangerous unbelief is. Many pious and self-righteous Christians look down their religious noses at people committing other, more visible sins. They criticize them sharply without realizing that the unbelief they harbor in their hearts, and in some cases enshrine in their doctrines, is more wicked in God's sight than the sins they are condemning. Jesus rebuked His disciples for unbelief more than any other thing. The reason unbelief is so dangerous is that not only is it a sin in itself, but it also can be a gateway for other sins as well.

> Satan knows that if he can inject unbelief into our spirits, he can effectively rob us of God's best for our lives. For this reason unbelief is a deadly enemy of God's plan for your life.

There have been many wonderful books written and many powerful sermons preached about faith. Indeed, faith is the currency of God's kingdom, and without faith it is impossible to please God (Heb. 11:6). However, I think many people have a basic misunderstanding about faith. They pray and seek more and more faith. But what if I told you that you already have plenty of faith? The problem is not that you have too little faith; the problem is something else. What if I told you that your faith is already enough to move mountains? Many people will find this hard to accept, but it is very biblical.

In Mark 9:24 a man said to Jesus, "I do believe; help me overcome my unbelief!" (NIV). Notice that he didn't ask Jesus to give him more faith. In fact, he said, "I do believe." This man recognized that the problem was not *too little* faith but *too much* unbelief! Perhaps you don't see the distinction I am making here. Some people think unbelief simply means "no faith." But it is possible to be an unbelieving believer. In other words, faith and unbelief could be present at the same time. Faith has the potential to move mountains, but unbelief will nullify the power of faith. Let me explain it like this.

When my wife was still in Bible college, her father bought her a very special gift: a car! It was a brand-new, silver *diesel* Volkswagen Jetta. It was a wonderful car that served us well for a long time. One day she lent the car to a friend. On his way to return the car to us, as a courtesy he decided to refill the fuel he had used. He pulled into the gas station, inserted his credit card, opened the cap of the gas tank, and began to fill it—with *gasoline*! How he missed the bold red warning on the tank that said to use "DIESEL FUEL ONLY" I will never know. But one thing is certain; his little mistake was costly for us and devastating for the vehicle.

After the gasoline was added, the vehicle would no longer run. It's not that there was too little diesel in the tank. The problem was the injection of a substance that was incompatible with the vehicle's design. This is exactly how unbelief works. The devil wants to inject unbelief into our spirits because he knows it will bring us to a screeching halt.

In Matthew 17:20 Jesus said, "If ye have faith as a grain of mustard seed, ye shall say unto this mountain, Remove hence to yonder place; and it shall remove; and nothing shall be impossible unto you." The mustard seed is the smallest of all seeds. Some would conclude that if faith as a grain of mustard seed can move mountains, then they must not have any faith at all, because so far they have been unable to move even a thimble. However, Romans 12:3 says God has given *everyone* a measure of faith.

> Faith has the potential to move mountains, but unbelief will nullify the power of faith.

It's true that some people have more of a measure of faith than others. Some have faith like an apple seed. Some have faith like a peach pit. And some people have the smallest measure of faith—like a mustard seed. But it doesn't really matter much because even if you have mustard seed faith, you still have enough to move mountains! So then some may ask, "What is the problem? Why haven't I seen the mountains in my own life moving out of my way?"

Let us consider the context of the verse where Jesus talked about mountain-moving faith. The story is found in Matthew 17:14–21. A certain man with a demon-possessed son had come to Jesus's disciples for help, but when they could not cast out the evil spirits, they asked Jesus why they had been so unsuccessful. He said to them, "Because of your unbelief" (v. 20). This is a very clear and precise explanation that Jesus reiterated by going on to say, "For verily I say unto you, If ye have faith as a grain of mustard seed, ye shall say unto this mountain, Remove hence to yonder place; and it shall remove; and nothing shall be impossible unto you" (v. 20). So far this seems very straightforward. But the simplicity and clarity of this statement is often overshadowed by confusion over the next words Jesus spoke: "Howbeit this kind goeth not out but by prayer and fasting" (v. 21).

It almost sounds as if Jesus contradicted Himself. When asked why the disciples had not been able to exorcize the demon, He said it was because of unbelief. But now He seems to be saying that it is because they had not fasted and prayed enough. Which is it? The confusion comes when we fail to realize the moral of the story. At first glance it may appear that the demon is the focal point of this account, but a closer look will reveal that the real antagonist in this story is not the demon but the spirit of unbelief. The disciples were concerned about the demon inside the boy, but Jesus was concerned about the unbelief inside His disciples. The disciples' question was about casting out demons, but Jesus's answer was about casting out doubt. Jesus knew that once unbelief has been cast out, exorcizing demons would be a piece of cake.

Sometimes we have to pray long prayers and fast for many days before we get the victory, but it is not because our appeals coerce God into doing something. And it is not because we have finally earned the answer to our prayers by logging enough credit hours into our spiritual bank account.

Much fasting and prayer may be necessary and useful in helping us gain victory over our own stubborn flesh and cast out the spirit of unbelief that blocks God's power from flowing through us. It is this kind of *unbelief* that goes out only "by prayer and fasting." It is also worth mentioning that some manuscripts do not contain the statement about prayer and fasting at all, which is why many Bible translations have left it out completely. Any way you look at it, faith is the key to powerful prayer. This is the point Jesus made in this story.

In Matthew 9:25, when Jairus's daughter died, Jesus had to send everyone out of the room before He could raise her from the dead. Why didn't He allow all those scornful skeptics to see the miracle with their own eyes? Because He had to cast the unbelief out. Peter did the same thing in Acts 9:40: "But Peter sent them all out and knelt down and prayed, and turning to the body, he said, 'Tabitha, arise.' And she opened her eyes, and when she saw Peter, she sat up"

(NAS). Jesus taught His disciples a lesson: Cast the spirit of unbelief out, and nothing will be able to stand against you. Demons, death, and even the most formidable mountains will obey your command.

Investors often "diversify" their investments because if one venture doesn't work out, they want to have something else to fall back on. So a common idiom in the business world is, "Don't put all your eggs in one basket." That means, don't put all your resources into one investment because if one of your "baskets" breaks and all your "eggs" are in it, you will lose everything. You see, if you are holding back some of your "eggs," it means you are not 100 percent confident that a particular basket will hold. You may be 50 percent confident or even 99 percent confident, but that small percentage of apprehension is what I am calling "unbelief." So how do you know when you've gotten rid of all the unbelief? When you've put all of your eggs into God's basket.

Early in ministry I came to a crossroads where I had to decide to go in one direction or another. I essentially had to choose between a situation that offered security, financially and otherwise, and following the call of God with all its risks and unknowns. I had an inward conviction that I had to give myself fully to one or the other, but I didn't want to let go of either option. In prayer I said, "Lord, I don't want to be foolish and put all of my eggs in one basket." Then I heard the Lord speak. He said, "You can trust My basket." I have seen this to be true. God's basket is the best one; it is fully reliable and never breaks.

When Hernán Cortés, the famous Spanish explorer, arrived in Mexico's harbor of Veracruz in 1519, he faced overwhelming odds. Before him lay the mighty Aztec Empire with its vast armies. But Cortés had only about six hundred men with him. They were far from home in a strange land; all possible odds were stacked hopelessly against them. Cortés knew his men would always have one eye on the ships, longing for home. He knew that in the back of their minds they would always be considering the highly attractive alternative of retreat. He knew that if these men were divided in heart or mind, the mission would surely fail.

So Cortés did something unthinkable. He ordered all eleven ships in their fleet to be burned. When the men stood on the shore and watched their only escape route going up in flames, it was a defining moment. There was no longer any possibility of turning back. They would either conquer or die. This consummate and unmitigated commitment unlocked unbelievable potential that gave them the power to succeed where all those before them had failed.

James 1:8 says, "A double minded man is unstable in all his ways." You will never really succeed at anything if you are halfway in and halfway out. If God has called you, it is not necessary to have a "backup plan." You don't need to hedge your bets. You don't need to hold some of your eggs back "just in case." Cast out the unbelief, put all your eggs in God's basket, burn your ships, and give yourself to Him and His plan, body, soul, and spirit.

When you are 100 percent committed and there is no turning back, you will break into a level of effectiveness and power that you've never experienced before. You will succeed where others have failed. You will overcome in the face of overwhelming odds. Mountains will move for you, and nothing will be impossible for you.

Chapter 14

ENEMY #4—THE SEDATIVE OF EXCUSES

JESUS SAID, "SEEK, and you will find" (Matt. 7:7, NKJV), and this is especially true of excuses. If you are looking for an excuse, you can always find one. Some people are too young. Some are too old. Some are not smart enough. Some are not experienced enough. Some are not privileged enough. Some don't have enough money. Some don't have the right abilities. For some it's not time yet; for others it's too late. Excuses are a penny a pound, plentiful and cheap—and God does not buy them!

We become extremely creative when we want to make an excuse. Our excuses can often sound very noble and even spiritual at times. We use excuses to fool others, but they are especially effective at helping us to fool ourselves. We use them as a sedative to soothe our conscience and to make us feel better about our own disobedience and laziness.

My friend, God has a wonderful plan for your life, and He invites you to partake of it, but excuses are a dangerous enemy that can keep you from possessing what God has for you. I have seen how excuses have kept so many wonderful people from realizing their

God-given potential. This is a great tragedy because life is so short, and time wasted can never be recovered.

This book has been written to help you discover God's will for your life, but the discovery of God's will for your life is never going to be enough in and of itself. Knowing God's will and fulfilling it are two entirely different things! The reality is that many people already know what God has called them to do. Even if they don't realize it or won't admit it, God has already revealed His will to them in one way or another. But they never achieve all that God has given to them to accomplish. And they never enter into the fullness of the blessings God has prepared for them because they comfort themselves in disobedience and laziness through excuses.

Although there are far too many excuses to mention, I would like to address a few that are especially common. As you read through the following list of excuses, I would like to challenge you to allow this to be a sort of diagnostic test. Examine your own heart to see if you are allowing these excuses, or others like them, to keep you from walking in the fullness of what God has for your life.

...but I'm Waiting on the Lord

This is one of those excuses that sounds so spiritual. Please don't misunderstand me. I'm not saying there is never a legitimate reason to wait on the Lord. But remember, we use excuses to soothe our own conscience, and the more sincere they sound, the better. Yes, there might be a legitimate time to wait on the Lord, but this can also be, and often is, nothing more than an excuse not to do what we already know to do.

In Exodus 14 the children of Israel had just come out of Egypt and had set their faces toward the Promised Land. But between the land of their captivity and the land of their destiny there was an obstacle that seemed insurmountable—the Red Sea. With no way to cross this body of water, they looked back toward Egypt and saw a cloud of dust stirred up by a thousand horses' hooves—and it was hurtling toward them. The armies of Pharaoh were on their way to wipe them off the face of the earth. As you can imagine, the children of Israel began to panic. They ran to Moses, their wise leader, for his advice, and these were his instructions:

> And Moses said to the people, "Do not be afraid. Stand still, and see the salvation of the LORD, which He will accomplish for you today. For the Egyptians whom you see today, you shall see again no more forever. The LORD will fight for you, and you shall hold your peace." And the LORD said to Moses, "Why do you cry to Me? Tell the children of Israel to go forward."
> —EXODUS 14:13–15, NKJV

"Stand still," Moses said, "and see the salvation of the Lord." Have you ever heard a sermon about standing still? I know I have. In fact, I have preached on this very subject in the past. And then one day I heard Evangelist Reinhard Bonnke speak about this passage in a way that changed my view forever. He said: "Facing the Red Sea on the one side and Pharaoh's army on the other, Moses said to the people, 'Fear ye not, stand still and see the salvation of the Lord' (v. 13). But God was not happy. He gave a *counter-command*: 'Speak unto the children of Israel, *that they go forward*' (v. 15, emphasis added). When you hear 'stand still,' it's Rev. Moses, but when you hear, 'Go forward,' it is God."

> The reality is that many people already know what God has called them to do....But they never...enter into the fullness of the blessings God has prepared for them because they comfort themselves in disobedience and laziness through excuses.

The word of the Lord is "Go forward!" Begin to move in the direction God is leading. Even God cannot steer a parked car! Get moving for God, and you will find that He will begin to guide your steps and direct your path.

...but I Don't Want to Get Ahead of God

This is another spiritual-sounding excuse, but to think that we can outrun God seems a bit silly to me. Can you imagine God in heaven huffing and puffing and leaning on Gabriel's shoulder as He says, "Man, I wish that guy would slow down. He's so quick I can hardly keep up with him!" More than likely God has been waiting on you to catch up rather than the other way around.

Any one of these points could be qualified with a list of caveats, but rather than thinking of all the instances when this concern could be legitimate, ask yourself, "Am I using this as an excuse in my life?" And if it is indeed an excuse, no matter how spiritual it sounds, you need to drop it and get moving in Jesus's name!

...but I Don't Have Enough Money

Financial needs are one of the most practical barriers to fulfilling our dreams. Many times the money issue boils down to a faith issue. We make excuses because we are not fully convinced that God will provide for our needs. The next few sentences will change your life and even your destiny if you will allow them to sink deep into your heart.

God is not poor, and He has no need of anything. When He orders something, He will *always* pay for it, and He never expects us to finance His will on our own. When God wants something, He never asks "How much?" because cost is no issue to Him. The only thing that governs what God can or cannot do in our lives is our willingness to believe Him, trust Him, and obey Him. Never decide what is or isn't God's will in your life by looking at the money that is or isn't in your pocket. Check God's pockets! They are filled with more than enough!

I realize that not everyone reading this book is called into "full-time ministry," but let me take a moment to speak to those who are, because for them the matter of finances is perhaps one of the biggest challenges and sources of confusion. Ministry today is often viewed as a profession. We have been reminded quite often that "the labourer is worthy of his hire" (Luke 10:7) and that we should not muzzle the ox when he is working (Deut. 25:4). When I preach about the call of God into the ministry, the first thing most people think of are paid positions, and they immediately begin to wonder about what level of financial support they might find. It seems many people automatically think of "ministry" as a paying "full-time job," and I wonder sometimes how much interest there would be if there were no possibility of financial reward.

When God sent Malachi to Jerusalem shortly after the temple had been rebuilt, he was appalled by the apathy of the people and especially of the "clergy." He observed that the priests seemed to be motivated by what they could get out of their service rather than by sincere love for God and a desire to build His kingdom. They were hirelings and mercenaries working for pay. God wondered if anyone would still be there to light the fires on the altar or even shut the doors if there were no promise of financial compensation (Mal. 1:10). I have no problem with ministers who make a living from their work in the ministry. In fact, I am one of them. But if financial remuneration becomes the incentive or prerequisite for ministry, there is a real problem.

I started preaching when I was fourteen years old, and ever since then I have always worked in "the ministry" in many different capacities. Most of the time I have been in ministry, it has been totally volunteer and has even cost me dearly. I have had to work secular jobs to support my family. Even as a senior pastor I took no salary and never felt entitled to anything.

If there were no money in ministry, I would still be doing it today and for the rest of my life. Why? Because I love Jesus and because it is what He has called me to do. I cannot imagine not ministering.

Ministry is not my job—it is my life. I *am* a minister—it's not just what I do. I am amazed sometimes to think that today I am able to make a living doing something that I love so much.

Jesus told His disciples, "My food is to do the will of Him who sent Me" (John 4:34, NAS). This is reward enough. It is remuneration enough. And then He gave this exhortation: "Do not work for the food which perishes, but for the food which endures to eternal life" (John 6:27, NAS). As ministers we work not for money or for food; we work for Jesus. Money will follow ministry, and as we seek first the kingdom of God, all these things will be added to us.

There are many people who wait until "they can afford it" to do the thing God has called them to do. They have somehow convinced themselves that funding God's will for their lives is *their* responsibility. They're wrong about that. It's *God's* responsibility, and He is more than happy to take care of it. In the meantime do what He is calling you to do, in whatever way you can, and stop using money as an excuse.

…but I Don't Have Enough (Talent, Experience, Education, Intelligence, etc.)

Whenever I hear people use these excuses, it reminds me of when God called Moses in Exodus 3. The Lord appeared to Moses in a flame of fire out of the midst of a burning bush and said, "Come now therefore, and I will send thee unto Pharaoh, that thou mayest bring forth my people the children of Israel out of Egypt" (v. 10). Immediately Moses's mind filled with excuses—all the things he didn't have and couldn't do.

Moses was not a general—he was a shepherd. He was not a polished orator—he had a stuttering tongue. He was not equipped to lead a nation—he had his hands full leading a flock of sheep. How could he possibly do what God was asking him to do? "Who am I," Moses asks, "that I should go unto Pharaoh, and that I should bring forth the children of Israel out of Egypt?" (Exod. 3:11). And here we see Moses's mistake. He made the error of thinking it was about him—about his talents, abilities, and gifts. But God quickly corrects Moses over and over throughout the rest of the chapter:

- "I *am* the God of your father" (Exod. 3:6, NAS, emphasis added).

- "I *will* send you to Pharaoh" (Exod. 3:10, NAS, emphasis added).

- "Certainly I *will* be with thee" (Exod. 3:12, emphasis added).

- "I *am* that I am" (Exod. 3:14, emphasis added).

- "I *will* bring you up" (Exod. 3:17, emphasis added).

- "I *will* stretch out *my* hand" (Exod. 3:20, emphasis added).

- "I *will* give this people favour" (Exod. 3:21, emphasis added).

By the end of the conversation Moses had learned a very valuable lesson. The great I am is the Great "I *will*." God is the fulfiller of His Word. He is not looking for the most talented, the most intelligent, the most beautiful, the most articulate, the most educated, or the most charismatic. He is looking for those who will follow, who will yield, and who will obey.

If you don't feel qualified for one reason or another, take courage from the disciples. When Jesus chose them, He didn't go to the University of Jerusalem. He didn't select the brightest young minds from the synagogue. He went down to the fishing docks and chose some roughneck fishermen. This motley group of ragtag laymen was certainly not the "cream of the crop," but Jesus made a deal with them. Jesus said, "If you will follow Me, I *will* make you." (See

Matthew 4:19.) My friend, that is the same deal Jesus makes with every one of us. If we will follow Him, He will make us.

Following Jesus is so simple because you don't need to know the way. You don't need to be the miracle worker. You don't need to be the savior. You don't need to be the healer. Your job is to stop making excuses, let Him lead, do whatever He tells you to do, and follow!

...but I'm Not Ready Yet

Delayed obedience is disobedience! I have found this to be one of the most common reasons people fall short of the will of God in their lives. So many people are continuously waiting for the "right time" before they step out and do what God has called them to do. Reinhard Bonnke once told me, "Those who forever seek the will of God are overrun by those who do it."

We all recognize that there are times and seasons in God and that sometimes God will tell us to wait. We can't be impetuous and go off the deep end, doing whatever we please, whenever we please, and just hope God will somehow work it all out. That can prove to be a fatal mistake! But it can be just as big a mistake to wait and wait forever until everything is just right before we act. When God speaks to us, no matter what we think, we must obey because it is He, not us, who always knows the right time. As I said before, even God can't steer a parked car! The enemy will see to it that there are imperfect circumstances in our lives if he knows we will just keep waiting and waiting until the timing seems perfect. We must allow the Holy Spirit, not our circumstances, to determine what that right time is.

In Luke 9:59–60 we read the story of someone whom Jesus called to follow Him: "And he said unto another, Follow me. But he said, Lord, suffer me first to go and bury my father. Jesus said unto him, Let the dead bury their dead: but go thou and preach the kingdom of God."

I've known this scripture for as far back as I can remember, and I must confess that for most of my life I did not understand what was going on here. In the back of my mind I had this feeling that Jesus was not fair to that poor young man. The man had not responded negatively to Jesus's call. He didn't say, "No, Lord, I will not follow You." Actually he was quite positive and made only a simple request, "Lord, suffer me first to go and bury my father." Was this so much to ask? After all, which of us would not want to attend our father's funeral? Which of us wouldn't want one day off to bury a dead loved one? Which of us would not have made the same request if one of our parents had just died?

One day I was reading this passage over and over, trying to understand it. Finally I put my Bible down and said, "Lord, why were You so impatient with that young man? Why couldn't You have given him one extra day to bury his dead father?" The Holy Spirit spoke to my heart so clearly. Rather than answering my question, He asked me a question of His own. He said, "What makes you think this man's father was dead?" I looked at the passage again and realized it does not say anywhere that the father had died. It says only that this young man wanted to wait to follow Jesus until he had a chance to bury his father.

My eyes were opened, and suddenly I realized what was happening here. This young man wanted to put off obedience to the call of Jesus until a more convenient time. Perhaps his father was old and surely would not live much longer. The young man thought, "After my father is dead, that will be a much more convenient time to follow Jesus." He probably figured Jesus would be around for the next fifty years preaching and teaching. Surely he had plenty of time. But within three years Jesus would go to the cross, and the chance to walk with Him and learn from Him one on one would have passed forever. This young man had no idea how precious, how rare, and how fleeting was this invitation. He missed the opportunity of his lifetime because of two costly little words: "But first." Can you see it? This is what so many of us do!

Jesus comes to us, perhaps in our youth, and He says, "Follow Me." We say, "Yes, Lord, I will follow You, but first let me finish my education."

Time goes by, we graduate, and then He comes to us again. "Follow Me," He says. We answer, "Yes, Lord, I will follow You, but first let me get a job and save up some money so I have something to fall back on."

We get a job, time goes by, and He comes to us again. "Follow Me," He says. We say, "Yes, Lord, I will follow You, but first let me put my kids through school."

The kids grow, leave the house, and have children of their own. He comes to us again, "Follow Me." We say, "Yes, Lord, I will follow You, but first let me retire from my job so I can collect my pension."

The years fly by faster than we expected. The young become old, and soon life has been spent. One day they lower our bodies into the earth to return to dust, and in the end so many never followed God's call. My friend, the greatest tragedy in the world is a wasted life. Real life, in its fullest sense, is not merely having a pulse but doing the will of God. Many are dead while they live. "Let the dead bury their dead," Jesus said, "but go thou and preach the kingdom of God" (Luke 9:60).

We are all familiar with the twelve disciples. These were the ones who responded to Jesus's call. But I wonder how many people did not respond. This young man might have been disciple number thirteen. There might have been a book of the Bible named after him. His name might have been one of those written on the foundations in the New Jerusalem, but today we do not know his name. We know only of his epic missed opportunity. Let's see the difference between his response to Christ's call and the response of those who actually became Jesus's disciples.

Matthew 4:18–22 gives the account of Peter's and Andrew's

call. "Now as Jesus was walking by the Sea of Galilee, He saw two brothers, Simon who was called Peter, and Andrew his brother, casting a net into the sea; for they were fishermen. And He said to them, 'Follow Me, and I will make you fishers of men.' *Immediately* they left their nets and followed Him. Going on from there He saw two other brothers, James the son of Zebedee, and John his brother, in the boat with Zebedee their father, mending their nets; and He called them. *Immediately* they left the boat and their father, and followed Him" (NAS, emphasis added).

I love the way Luke describes this same event in his Gospel. "And when they had brought their ships to land," he says, "they forsook all, and followed him" (Luke 5:11). *Immediately* they left their nets. *Immediately* they left their boats. They forsook everything and they followed Jesus. What a response! Something stirs in my soul when I read this. I want to jump up with those men and abandon everything to follow the Lamb wherever He goes. This is what that other

> When Jesus calls, He doesn't mean, "Get back to Me sometime today." He means answer *now*! Don't procrastinate! Delayed obedience is disobedience.

unnamed young man was missing. It was not for him to decide when was the right time to obey. He should have immediately forsaken everything and answered the call.

Procrastination is the devil's best friend. The devil knows that delayed obedience is disobedience. The devil knows "tomorrow" never comes. Many people have missed salvation not because they rejected it, but because the devil convinced them to just put it off for a little while. He convinced young people that they have plenty of time. He convinced others to wait because of relationships or pet sins they were not ready to forsake. The devil knows there will never be a more perfect opportunity to follow Jesus than when He calls.

Have you ever heard someone quote the verse that says, "Today is the day of salvation"? Actually there is no such verse in the Bible. Second Corinthians 6:2 actually says, *"Now* is the day of salvation" (emphasis added). To say "today is the day" is not urgent enough. The time is *now!* If a person is drowning, he doesn't need to be rescued sometime today. He needs to be rescued *now!* When Jesus calls, He doesn't mean "get back to Me sometime today." He means answer *now!* Don't procrastinate! Don't wait! Respond immediately, forsake everything that holds you back, and follow Jesus! Delayed obedience is disobedience.

Let me take a moment to especially address those who have the evangelistic calling as I do. Jesus said to that young man in Luke 9:60, "Let the dead bury their dead: but go thou and preach the kingdom of God." When it comes to God's will for your life, this matter of answering God's call is especially urgent for those who have been called to preach the gospel.

Imagine that you are a doctor. In fact, you are the best doctor in the whole country, and there is a deadly plague sweeping through. All around you people are dying left and right. You are the only one who knows how to cure the disease. You are the only one who has the vaccine. You are rushing to the hospital to save hundreds of patients who are on their deathbeds when someone on the side of the road calls out, "Hey, you. Come over here and help us bury these dead bodies." You would reply, "I'm sorry. I cannot help you. I'm too busy saving lives to bury bodies."

My friend, we have the most critical of all mandates. All around us people are perishing by the millions. We have the answer for the plague of sin and death. "Dear children," John said, "this is the last hour" (1 John 2:18, NIV). The need could not be more urgent, and the time could not be more appropriate. There are a lot of good causes that need someone's attention, but none are more important than the call to preach the gospel. We need to let someone else do the "good" things while we stay focused on the most important thing—winning souls! We are not called to bury the dead—we are called to raise the dead!

The Call vs. the Commission

Allow me to become extremely practical at this point, if I may. I once preached about answering the call with urgency, and afterward someone came up to me and said, "God called me to the mission field, but you said I should obey now. Does this mean I should quit my job and move to another country right away?" These particulars are where matters become very personal and highly customized. Ultimately only you can know what God is saying to you, and only you will be accountable to God. But for most people I think it's safe to say that when God calls you, He doesn't expect you to go to the airport immediately or sail with the next tide.

This may sound like a contradiction of what I previously said, but if there is any confusion about this point, it is because of a failure to distinguish between the "call" and the "commission." When Jesus called His disciples, He didn't call them to be apostles, prophets, evangelists, pastors, or teachers. He simply called them to follow Him. And as they followed Him, Jesus promised that He would "make" them into "fishers of men." Now the disciples left their nets immediately to follow Jesus, but they were not made into fishers of men immediately. There was a season of training between when Jesus called them to follow Him and when He commissioned them to preach the gospel.

Obedience to the call of God is about following Jesus. If you have heard the call of Jesus and you think you need to be on the next plane to the mission field, then you probably misunderstood what He said when He called you. He probably didn't say, "Go and do." He most likely said, "Come and follow." Don't worry about the commission. It will come as you follow Jesus.

Chapter 15

ENEMY #5—THE WITCHCRAFT OF REBELLION

A FTER I FINISHED preaching recently, two young men appro-ached me. They said the Lord had called them to be evangelists, and they asked if I had any advice for them. I said, "Yes, I can give you my advice in one word: *obey!*" I think this is perhaps the single greatest word of advice anyone could have for discovering and remaining in God's will. Unfortunately it is also one of the areas of greatest difficulty for so many of God's people. We are like sheep—prone to wander and amazingly stupid. We are like donkeys—stubborn and willful. We are like peacocks—proud and vain. We are quick to analyze and rationalize but slow to obey. We are masters of procrastination and experts at justification. Making excuses comes naturally to us, but simple obedience seems so difficult.

> God is all knowing and all wise. When He speaks, He is giving you insider information for your advantage, and your obedience is the most profitable thing you could do for yourself.

"And now, Israel, what does the LORD your God require of you, but to fear the LORD your God, to walk in all His ways and to love Him, to serve the LORD your God with all your heart and with all your soul, and to keep the commandments of the LORD and His statutes which I command you today *for your good*?" (Deut. 10:12–13, NKJV, emphasis added). Notice that God's commands are not given to make us miserable; they are for our own good. This might sound like a cliché, but please do not dismiss it and simply go on to the next paragraph. Stop to consider this thought for a moment. God is all knowing and all wise. He knows the future. He knows the past. He can see what is ahead in your life and in the lives of everyone around you. He knows what is going to happen in the economy, in politics, and on the world stage. When He speaks, He is giving you insider information for your advantage, and your obedience is the most profitable thing you could do for yourself.

I could point to many examples in my own life of times when God spoke to me about something, but because obeying required some level of personal sacrifice, I struggled and wrestled in my own heart and mind, sometimes for far too long. In the end I discovered that His instructions were meant to save me mountains of heartache, pain, and expense. If we could only learn to obey, we would be fulfilled, happy, and blessed in every way. John H. Sammis's famous hymn says it well:

Trust and obey, for there's no other way
To be happy in Jesus, but to trust and obey.[1]

Consider Israel's first king, Saul, who always thought his idea was better than God's command. Each act of rebellion led him deeper into trouble and farther from God's will. It was to Saul that Samuel said, "Has the LORD as great delight in burnt offerings and sacrifices, as in obeying the voice of the LORD? Behold, to obey is better than sacrifice, and to heed than the fat of rams. For rebellion is as the sin of witchcraft, and stubbornness is as iniquity and idolatry. Because you have rejected the word of the LORD, He also has rejected you from being king" (1 Sam. 15:22–23, NKJV).

Just as rebellion blocks God's blessings, so obedience releases them. Consider the widow of Zarephath, who experienced an extraordinary miracle of provision. A terrible famine was ravaging the land. God spoke to Elijah in 1 Kings 17:9 and said, "Arise, get thee to Zarephath…behold, I have commanded a widow woman there to sustain thee." Notice that God did not send Elijah to a woman living in a mansion with huge storehouses of grain from which she could provide for the prophet. Instead, the Lord sent him to a poor widow who didn't have enough food to provide for her own family.

I emphasize this because God could have sent Elijah to anyone. For that matter He could have continued to send ravens to feed him. The point is that Elijah didn't really need this woman's food. God didn't send Elijah to the woman so that He could provide for Elijah. God sent Elijah to the widow so He could provide for the widow. Why would the Lord command a poor widow to make such a costly sacrifice? It must have seemed cruel and senseless. But it was for her own good! Her obedience unlocked a fountain of provision that she could never have anticipated. "The bowl of flour was not exhausted nor did the jar of oil become empty, according to the word

> There is no alternative to obedience—not even sacrifices, invocations, or tears. When God speaks, there is only one appropriate response—immediate, unquestioning obedience.

of the LORD which He spoke through Elijah" (1 Kings 17:16, NAS).

There is favor, prosperity, peace, joy, and blessing for those who obey, but the rebellious reap the reward of their own ways. In Colossians 3:6 unbelievers are called "the children of disobedience," and it says the wrath of God comes upon them. We are not the children of disobedience, but we are known by a different characteristic. In John 10:27 Jesus said, "My sheep listen to my voice; I know them, and they follow me" (NIV). One way God's people are distinguished from the lost is by their obedience to His voice.

Have you ever stopped to consider how sinful disobedience is? All of creation—galaxies, planets, tides, nature—everything obeys His command, everything except people. Perhaps the greatest sin of humanity is the sin of self-will. I love the way missionary Paul Washer illustrated this point in a recent sermon. He said: "Imagine this. Here stands God on the day of creation. He looks at stars that could swallow up a thousand of our suns. He looks at them and He says, 'All you stars, move yourself to this place and start in this order and move in a circle, and move exactly as I tell you until I give you another word.' And they all obey him. He says, 'Planets, pick yourself up and whirl. Make this formation at My command until I give you another word.' He looks at mountains and He says, 'Be lifted up,' and they obey Him. He tells valleys, 'Be cast down,' and they obey Him. He looks at the sea and says, 'You will come this far,' and the sea obeys, and then He looks at you and says, 'Come.' And you go, 'No!'"[2]

I've chosen to end this section about the enemies of God's will for your life with this chapter about rebellion because, at the end of the day, disobedience is at the core of all these enemies. Laziness, fear, unbelief, and excuses are all easily overcome if we will simply resolve in our hearts to obey no matter what. Rebellion is not only an enemy of God's will for your life; it is also a sign of a serious heart issue. God views rebellion and stubbornness as witchcraft, iniquity, and idolatry! There is no alternative to obedience—not even sacrifices, invocations, or tears. When God speaks, don't waste your time praying about it. When God speaks, don't waste your time rationalizing or analyzing His word. When God speaks, there is only one appropriate response—immediate, unquestioning obedience.

There are many people who have been praying about God's will and studying His Word, seeking His will, but God has already spoken, and they have yet to obey. This is called rebellion, and it will block God's blessings from flowing into your life. If you are not going to obey, none of the other advice in this book will help you. In fact, if you won't obey, even the Bible won't help you. As Martin Luther once said, "You may as well quit reading and hearing the Word of God, and give it to the devil, if you do not desire to live according to it."[3]

PART 4

FIVE LINGERING QUESTIONS ABOUT GOD'S WILL

Chapter 16

IF I ENCOUNTER RESISTANCE, AM I OUT OF GOD'S WILL?

WE'VE ALL HEARD clichés such as, "Where God guides He provides" or "What God ordains He sustains." And while there is an element of truth in trite adages such as these, they can often give a false impression that if someone is in God's will, everything will be easy. This misunderstanding can cause a person to constantly question God's call and His will. What happens when the bank account is empty and challenges arise on every side? Do we then conclude that God is not with us? Should we turn back or quit when the going gets rough?

Following the call of God does not guarantee that we will not encounter difficulties and hardships. In fact, the reality is quite the opposite. Jesus told His disciples in John 16:33, "In this world you will have trouble" (NIV). Paul said in 2 Timothy 3:12 that everyone who lives a godly life will suffer. But in the midst of the suffering there is peace, and every difficulty we encounter shapes our character and brings us closer to God.

Many people are familiar with the verse "And we know that all things work together for good to them that love God, to them who are the called according to his purpose" (Rom. 8:28). But many do not realize that when the apostle Paul penned those words, he was actually talking about suffering and hardships. He was saying that even these difficulties work together for our good if we love God and *are called according to His purpose.* Being in God's will does not guarantee that we will evade trouble and adversity, but it does guarantee that every trial we face will be an agent of God's love, actively working for our good in the end!

> Following the call of God does not guarantee that we will not encounter difficulties and hardships. In fact, the reality is quite the opposite.

The Scriptures are full of stories about "wilderness" experiences great men and women of God endured. The accounts of their hardships and difficulties are not simply incidental digressions. They are central elements of their stories because God used the wilderness to transform these ordinary people into heroes of the faith.

Jesus in the Wilderness of Temptation

In Luke 4 we read about the temptation of Jesus in the wilderness. Verse 1 says, "And Jesus being full of the Holy Ghost returned from Jordan, and was led by the Spirit into the wilderness." As I have already pointed out, Jesus was *not* led into the wilderness by the devil. The verse says He was led into the wilderness by the *Spirit!* Many times when we find ourselves in a wilderness experience, we immediately begin rebuking the devil. But it may actually be God leading us into the wilderness. Why would God do this to us? Why would He do this to Jesus? It is because of the next thing I would like to point out in Luke's rendition of the temptation story.

Luke 4:1 says that when Jesus went into the wilderness, he went in "full of the Holy Ghost." But at the end of the story, when Jesus came out of the wilderness, it says, He "returned *in the power of the Spirit*" (v. 14, emphasis added). There is something about the wilderness that produces powerful men and women of God. The wilderness is God's training ground, and it is often a prerequisite for promotion! Even Jesus had to go through it.

It is one thing to be filled with the Holy Spirit and have the potential to do great things for God. It is another thing altogether to have walked through the valley of the shadow of death and to emerge victorious on the other side. There is a big difference between an army cadet in basic training and a battle-hardened veteran, between a new recruit and a war hero who has been tested and tried and has earned his stripes and scars with valor. When you have been through the crisis of faith and experienced God's provision and power, when He has brought you up out of the miry pit and set your feet on the rock, when He has proven His faithfulness to you over and over again, you will emerge from the wilderness knowing and walking in the power of the Holy Spirit that is within you.

David in the Wilderness of Waiting

David was not a favorite candidate for greatness. He was not his father's first choice. In fact, when Samuel came to anoint a king from Jesse's house, David's father didn't even bother to call him out of the field. Instead he presented his older, more impressive sons to the prophet. But God's choice is often different from man's choice because while man looks at the outward appearance, God looks at the heart. God found David in the field, faithfully watching his sheep and worshipfully playing his harp. Against all human logic God chose David to be the next king of Israel. But before David could sit on the throne, he would have to go to the wilderness.

King Saul, possessed by evil spirits and plagued by cruel jealousy, hated David with unrelenting passion and hunted him like a bird (Lam. 3:52). David fled south toward the Dead Sea into the barren desert land where water is scarce and life is precious. There he hid in caves and ran from Saul for eight long years. David had been anointed the next king of Israel, yet he was hiding like an animal in a hole. It would have been easy for David to question God's plan during the desert years, but God used the scorching heat, the salty air, and the pelting sandstorms to forge a king from a shepherd boy in the lonely suffering of the wilderness. When David emerged from that barren wasteland, he ascended to a throne and an eternal covenant with the living God.

Moses in the Wilderness of Brokenness

Moses was chosen by God to be Israel's deliverer. He was protected from an infanticidal massacre and then adopted into the royal family of Egypt. He grew up in Pharaoh's palace, eating first-class delicacies, learning from Egypt's foremost tutors, and enjoying the finest luxuries. One look at this strapping young prince, and anyone could see that he was the perfect choice for a grand assignment. But this fine young man, ideal by every human standard, lacked one prerequisite for his providential mission. So God enrolled him in the school of brokenness and sent him to the wilderness, where Moses spent the next forty years of his life.

> Being in God's will does not guarantee that we will evade trouble and adversity, but it does guarantee that every trial we face will be an agent of God's love, actively working for our good in the end!

Sometimes God has to break us down so He can rebuild us His way. And often the more impressive the edifice of our own making, the longer and more painful is the process of dying to self and surrendering to God. Moses ran into the wilderness as a proud prince and came out as a humble prophet. He may have thought his life was over the day he escaped to the barren backside of the desert, but little did he know this would mark a new beginning. Forty years of wilderness wanderings would culminate in a fateful conversation with a burning bush that would change the course of history. It was this meekest of men to whom God spoke face-to-face as a man speaks with his friend and guided with fire and cloud. It was this stuttering vagabond to whom God gave tablets of stone that He engraved with His own finger. It was this wanted fugitive whose face shone with the glory of God when he came down from Mount Sinai. It was this broken prince who was used to part a sea and deliver an entire nation from slavery.

Israel in the Wilderness of Purging

God needed only one day to take Israel out of Egypt but forty years to take Egypt out of Israel. That's right—God took the whole nation through the wilderness before bringing Israel into her inheritance. Are you beginning to see a pattern here? Between Egypt and Canaan, the land of captivity and the land of destiny, there is always a process and a journey that leads through a dry, lonely, barren land. In that place God accomplishes an eternal and enduring work in our lives that will bring glory to His name.

How we would love to avoid the wilderness. We would opt out of the trial by fire if given an alternative. Yet these minor notes make the symphony of our lives, and of history, rich and beautiful in the end. Think of every story that has inspired you and every memory you hold dear. You will notice that every victory has been preceded by a battle, and every climax has been prefaced by a conflict. The testimony everyone wants to have includes a test no one wants to endure. The story everyone would love to tell contains a wilderness everyone wants to avoid. But talk with those who have gone through the trial by fire and have come forth as gold, and you will hear them say time and time again, "I wouldn't trade that experience for the world."

Pleasure over pain is our default setting, and we are usually looking for the path of least resistance. But unlike us God sees our lives from the vantage point of eternity, and His primary concern is not our comfort but our conforming to the image of His Son. How effective do you think an army would be if the soldiers were trained at five-star resorts? How reliable would a scholar be if he never took a test? How long would a boxer last in the ring if his training consisted of pillow fights?

I read about a scientific experiment that involved a group of researchers who had isolated themselves from the outside world in an artificial environment called a "biosphere." Inside the biosphere the scientists had successfully replicated nearly every weather condition on earth except for one—wind. To their surprise the absence of wind was disastrous for the trees, which began to bend and snap under their own weight. It turns out that wind strengthens the trees by creating stress. Without this resistance the trees will not develop enough strength to hold themselves upright. Douglas Malloch's poem "Good Timber" expresses this point brilliantly:

> The tree that never had to fight
> For sun and sky and air and light,
> But stood out in the open plain
> And always got its share of rain,
> Never became a forest king
> But lived and died a scrubby thing.
>
> The man who never had to toil
> To heaven from the common soil,
> Who never had to win his share
> Of sun and sky and light and air,
> Never became a manly man
> But lived and died as he began.
>
> Good timber does not grow in ease;
> The stronger wind, the tougher trees;
> The farther sky, the greater length;
> The more the storm, the more the strength.
> By sun and cold, by rain and snows,
> In trees and men, good timbers grow.

Where thickest stands the forest growth,
We find the patriarchs of them both.
And they hold converse with the stars
Whose broken branches show the scars
Of many winds and of much strife—
This is the common law of life.[1]

Several years ago when our kids were still toddlers, my wife and I lived in a house with a swimming pool that we enjoyed very much. But I was always concerned that one of the children might fall into the pool when an adult was not looking. So out of concern for their safety I enrolled my son and daughter in swimming lessons. The first few days were a torment, for them and for us, because learning to swim is a baptism by fire. I am sure my kids thought their teacher was trying to drown them. They cried, they resisted, they protested, and they pleaded for deliverance. But when they looked at us, their parents, we were sitting on the sidelines silently.

We watched their struggle, and our hearts were aching to see their distress, but we would not intervene. This challenge was for their own good, and we allowed it because of our love for them. But all the time they were struggling and suffering, our loving eyes were trained on them. We watched their every movement and would never have allowed them to drown.

Just before Moses died he sang a song over Israel and said, "He [*the Lord*] found him [*Israel*] in a desert land, in the howling void of the wilderness; He kept circling around him, He scanned him [penetratingly], He kept him as the pupil of His eye" (Deut. 32:10, AMP). Moses, Israel, David, and countless others—including Jesus Himself—passed through the wilderness as they followed the call of God. The difficulties they encountered and the trials they faced were all a part of God's plan and were used to accomplish God's purpose for their lives.

Being in God's will does not mean there will never be setbacks or that we will be immune to difficulty. But even in the midst of the wilderness God will spread His wings over us and keep circling around us as an eagle flutters over her young. He will keep us as the apple of His eye, and He will never allow us to drown.

Chapter 17

HOW DO I GET FROM WHERE I AM TO WHERE GOD WANTS ME TO BE?

IN THE LOBBY of our ministry's headquarters in Orlando, Florida, we have an enormous picture covering an entire wall that shows a vast crowd at one of our African evangelistic campaigns. People are often overwhelmed by the photo because it gives a small glimpse of the size of these massive events. It is especially inspiring to other evangelists who have been called, as we are, to reach as many people as possible with the gospel. One day a young evangelist was visiting the office, and he stood in front of that picture for the longest time just staring. Finally he pointed to the picture and said, "I've just been trying to figure out how to get to *that* from where I am now."

> If your dream really came from God, absolutely everything you need is going to be provided as you move forward.

I think this is a common question. How do we get from where we are at the moment to where we know God is calling us? If this is where you are, you are in a good place, even if it doesn't seem that way right now. You are in the place of having a dream that has been sent from heaven. If this dream really came from God, absolutely everything you need is going to be provided as you move forward. This is going to be the most amazing adventure of your life.

God has spoken, and He is going to do His part, but what is our role in this? We need to recognize that every journey begins with a small, single step. Walking into all God has for us in the future begins with us taking small steps in faith now. Ask yourself these three questions:

What Steps Can I Take to Prepare Myself?

Perhaps you've heard of someone who became an overnight success. The reality is that these sudden sensations are usually just an illusion. Someone told me, "It took me thirty years of hard work to become an overnight success." The truth is, when you see someone who appears to be an overnight success, what you are usually seeing is the intersection of preparation and opportunity. It is true that great opportunities come, but only those who are prepared will be able to take advantage of them. So what can you do to prepare yourself for the opportunity God is going to bring your way?

> Every journey begins with a small, single step. Walking into all God has for us in the future begins with us taking small steps in faith now.

Maybe God has called you to the nations to preach the gospel, but you don't have any preaching invitations. If I were you, I would get my passport, buy a suitcase, and start preparing some evangelistic messages so that when the opportunity presents itself for you to move forward, you are prepared. What opportunities do you have right now that are in line with what God is calling you to do? What is in your hand right now? Is there anything you need to do? Think about it. Is God calling you to go to school and get an education that will prepare you to fulfill the vision He has given you?

Go online today and start researching schools. Has He given you a dream of starting a business? Think of people you can talk with who have experience as entrepreneurs. Do you need to get healthy and lose some weight before you can do what God has called you to do? Change your eating habits and start a rigorous program of exercise right now. Just do something. Do anything. It may seem totally meaningless at the present time, but do it anyway. Even a small seed planted in faith can become the inception of fulfilling what God has called you to do.

How Can I Respond in Faith?

Ever since our ministry, Christ for all Nations, was incorporated in the United States in 1987, we have never owned any property here because we always felt it was our mandate to fast-track all available funds to the mission field—to invest in souls rather than bricks and mortar. We were renting offices in Orlando and were very content with what the Lord had provided. But several months ago on a Saturday morning, I received a call from our founder, Evangelist Reinhard Bonnke. He said, "The Lord spoke to me this morning and said that He has a 'Harvest Home' for us in Orlando."

Evangelist Bonnke believed God wanted to give us a facility of our own. The problem was, we didn't have a penny in any sort of building fund and had never even considered such a project. But Reverend Bonnke was sure the Lord had spoken, so he said, "I am coming to Orlando, and I want to meet with you right now." He drove two hours to meet with several of us about the "Harvest Home" that Saturday morning. Obviously nothing could have been done at that very moment. Even if God had spoken, much groundwork, research, and due diligence had to be done.

When I asked Evangelist Bonnke why he was in such a hurry to meet, he said, "I feel that the eyes of God are on me, and I want Him to see that when He speaks, I jump." Over the next few weeks we were witnesses to a miracle, as literally every penny for the purchase of a brand-new, state-of-the-art facility was provided supernaturally! I saw a direct correlation between Evangelist Bonnke's wholehearted response to God's word and His dramatic supply of our miracle.

If God has revealed His will to you but you are not sure exactly what to do—do *something*! Let God see that you take His word seriously and that when He speaks, you respond. As I have already mentioned, even God can't steer a parked car! You need to give Him something to work with. There are so many people who seek God's will, find it, and then never see it manifest in their lives because they were never willing to take any kind of action.

Some people are waiting for God to do everything for them. Some people have an attitude that says, "If this vision is from God, then it will just happen on its own." But my friend, it doesn't work that way! In Matthew 6:26 Jesus said, "Look at the birds of the air; they do not sow or reap or store away in barns, and yet your heavenly Father feeds them" (NIV). Yes, it's true, God provides for the birds of the air, but He doesn't build their nests for them or gather their food for them. They must spread their wings, and they must do their part. If you are sitting at home waiting for God to spoon-feed His will to you, you are going to be waiting for a very long time. You'd better spread your wings and get moving in faith and obedience. Show God that when He speaks, you jump!

What Can I Do to Move in the Direction of God's Call?

If you are in a dark room and you hear someone off to one side calling your name, the way to find the person is by moving in the direction the voice is coming from. This is so obvious, but it is amazing to me how many people sense God calling them to one particular area, yet everything they are doing is moving them in a different direction.

For example, if you are called to be a doctor, you should not be enrolling in law school. If you are called to the mission field, you should not be buying a big house in your hometown. If you are called to be a pastor, you should not be marrying someone who hates church.

Make sure that whatever you are doing is moving you closer to your call. For example, Joe feels God has called him to start a franchise of restaurants and use the profits to support missions. But he works as a car salesman and doesn't have the money to start his business right now. So how could Joe begin to move in the direction of God's call?

First of all, he could start giving to missions now, even if it's in small amounts. People often tell me that they are on the verge of a big business deal, and when they make their millions they are going to support our mission in Africa. But if they are not already giving of what they have at the moment, I highly doubt anything will change when and if they make their millions. What's more, God is not looking for people who have good intentions for what they will do *if* He blesses them. Rather, He is looking to bless people who are *already* being faithful and obedient with what they have.

The next thing Joe could do is to get a job that will position him closer to what God has called him to do. A job in the hospitality field would provide him with experience and contacts he will not get as a car salesman. If Joe really feels God is calling him to start and manage a restaurant chain, then he should immerse himself in that world, even if he has to take a pay cut and start as a janitor or a busboy.

Many people want God to lay out their future for them in advance like the blueprint of a building that is to be constructed. It never works out that way. Do not despise the day of small beginnings. Do not despise small steps as long as they are obedient, faith-filled steps that are moving you in the direction of God's call. As you move forward in obedience and faith, He is going to reveal it all, one step at a time.

Chapter 18

WHAT SHOULD I DO WHILE I'M SEEKING GOD'S WILL?

IT IS IMPORTANT to emphasize that the word *seek* is an action word. There are some people who say they are seeking God's will, but they are actually just waiting for a "lucky break." The question in this chapter is, "What should I do while I'm seeking God's will?" But the points I am about to outline are actually what I believe it means to seek God's will in the first place. These are not only things you can do while you're waiting for God to reveal His will for your life—if you are not doing these things, then you are not seeking God's will at all.

A person who is seeking God's will is actively asking for God's direction, looking for opportunities to use what is already in his hand, helping others fulfill their God-given visions, and being faithful wherever he finds himself at the moment.

Actively Ask for God's Direction

Are you asking God what He wants you to do? Are you listening for Him to lead you and guide you in everyday life? James 4:2 says, "Ye have not, because ye ask not." The importance of prayer may seem like an incredibly simple thing to mention, perhaps an insult to your intelligence. But you would be surprised to learn how many people have simply never taken the time to seriously pray about what God would have them to do. There are times when God will intentionally hold back something He wants to give you simply because you have not stopped to inquire of Him.

> A person who is seeking God's will is actively asking for God's direction, looking for opportunities to use what is already in his hand, helping others fulfill their God-given visions, and being faithful wherever he finds himself at the moment.

In my book titled *Your Kingdom Come: Unlocking the Miraculous Through Faith and Prayer* I have written in-depth on the topic of prayer and intercession. The following excerpt demonstrates a profound principle from the life of Asa, the king who dug his own grave:

> It's amazing how many people choose to involve God so little in their lives. When it comes to decisions about business, family, career and the weightier matters of life, they seek out qualified counsel, yet they never bend a knee before the King of the Universe who stands by longing to help them. He desires to be glorified through our lives, yet many times we deprive Him of that right.
>
> It is more than just unfortunate when we fail to inquire of the Lord. When we rob our Creator, Sustainer and Provider of His rightful place in our lives, it is literally offensive to God.
>
> Second Chronicles 16:9 AMP says, "For the eyes of the Lord run to and from throughout the whole earth to show Himself strong in behalf of those whose hearts are blameless toward Him." This is a verse that is often quoted in many different situations, but it may surprise you to learn the context of that verse and the fascinating circumstances

surrounding it. It is both an insight and an admonition for our own lives.

Baasha, the King of Israel, came up against Judah in war and tried to starve the people out by besieging them at Ramah. So Asa, the king of the besieged Judah, "brought silver and gold out of the treasuries of the house of the Lord and sent them to Ben-hadad king of Syria...saying, Let there be a league between me and you...break your league with Baasha king of Israel, that he may withdraw from me" (2 Chronicles 16:2–3 AMP).

The Syrians, whose allegiance Asa had bought with gold from the Lord's house, came down and rescued the southern kingdom from the hand of Baasha. It would seem like a happy ending, but the Lord was not pleased. God wanted to be Judah's defender and deliverer, but instead Asa had given that opportunity to the Syrians. In the same way, Asa had taken the gold from the Lord's house and given it to another; he had also taken the glory from the Lord and given it to another.

So God sent a prophet named Hanani to King Asa with this message, "...Because you relied on the king of Aram [Syria] and not on the LORD your God, the army of the king of Aram [Syria] has escaped from your hand. Were not the Cushites and Libyans a mighty army with great numbers of chariots and horsemen? Yet when you relied on the LORD, he delivered them into your hand. For the eyes of the LORD range throughout the earth to strengthen those whose hearts are fully committed to him. You have done a foolish thing, and from now on you will be at war" (2 Chronicles 16:7–9 NIV).

Because of fear, Asa chose to call upon, and put his trust in, the king of Syria rather than on the Lord, and God was offended. As a result of this, the Lord gave Asa over to the very thing he feared most, "...from now on you will be at war." By not including the Lord, Asa had actually brought upon himself the very thing he was trying to avoid. "It is better to trust in the LORD than to put confidence in man. It is better to trust in the LORD than to put confidence in princes" (Psalm 118:8–9).

How often has God stood by ready, willing and able to help us, but we never turned to Him or gave Him an opportunity to intervene and bring glory to Himself through our crisis? As a result, we have often forfeited peace and struggled under the load of unnecessary burdens—all because we did not inquire of the Lord. What's worse, an opportunity to bring glory to God was lost.

What is so amazing is that Asa makes the *very same mistake* again only three verses later: "In the thirty-ninth year of his reign Asa was diseased in his feet—until his disease became very severe; yet in his disease he did not seek the Lord, but relied on the physicians. And Asa slept with his fathers, dying in the forty-first year of his reign" (2 Chronicles 16:12–13 AMP).

Can you see the pattern? The author is trying to communicate a moral through this story that is of utmost importance. Asa called upon the help of foreign armies instead of the Lord, and as a result, he inherited perpetual war. He called on the aid of doctors instead of the Lord when he became sick, and as a result, he inherited death. God wanted to help Asa. God wanted to deliver him from his enemies. God wanted to heal him from his diseases. But for some strange reason, like so many of us, Asa ignored God in the issues that mattered most, and as a result, he sealed his own fate.

The final verse of the chapter sums Asa's life up with an almost contemptuous caption: "And they buried him in his own tomb *which he had hewn out for himself....*" (2 Chronicles 16:14 AMP). In essence, Asa dug his own grave and put the final nail in his own coffin because he insisted on calling upon the arm of flesh rather than on the Lord. God was insulted by Asa's disregard and gave him over to that which he feared most. Jeremiah 17:5 NAS says, "Thus says the LORD, 'Cursed is the man who trusts in mankind and makes flesh his strength, and whose heart turns away from the LORD.'"[1]

If you are seeking God's will for your life, it means that you are actively praying about it, waiting before the Lord, and listening for His direction. Perhaps you have not heard an answer because you haven't asked the question. Perhaps you have asked, but you haven't been listening. Maybe it's time to turn off the television, put away the video games, and spend some time on your knees before the Lord, reading His Word and listening to His voice. His promise is, "You will seek me and find me when you seek me with all your heart" (Jer. 29:13, NIV).

Use What Is Already in Your Hand

It is interesting that when people ultimately discover what God has called them to do, often they look back and see that God had placed many things in their lives early on to prepare them for their calling. It might have been a natural talent or ability. It might have been certain interests. It may have been people who influenced them in the direction of their calling, even if they didn't recognize

> If you are seeking God's will for your life, it means that you are actively praying about it, waiting before the Lord, and listening for His direction.

it at the time. It may have been an event or an experience that propelled them toward the plans God had for them. One thing is certain: God *always* prepares us for the things He has in store for us.

When God called Moses to deliver the children of Israel out of Egypt, Moses was thoroughly overwhelmed. His mind was filled with questions, and he could not even imagine how he would begin to accomplish such a feat. He began to bombard God with questions, concerns, and objections, but God did not say, "Don't worry, Moses. This is what I'm going to do. First, I'm going to turn the waters of the Nile into blood. Then I'll send a plague of frogs followed by a plague of lice followed by a plague of flies. Then I'll kill the livestock, send boils, hail and locusts, then follow that up with darkness and death of the firstborn. Once you're out of Egypt, I'll part the Red Sea and lead you through the wilderness with a pillar of cloud by day and a pillar of fire by night." I'm sure such a detailed revelation of God's plan would have been a great comfort to Moses. Instead when Moses asked all his frantic questions about how God would deliver His people, God responded with a question of His own. "Moses, what is in your hand?" And Moses replied, "A rod."

Think for a minute about the absurdity of what God was asking Moses to do. He was sending this fugitive vagabond into the most powerful empire in the world to deliver His people. And all Moses had as ammunition was a stick! Through the whole Exodus saga— all the miracles, wonders, and epic, world-changing exploits—Moses had nothing more in his hand than a stick! But when Moses did what he knew to do, when he used what was in his hand, the rest of the story began to unfold, each event triggering the next like a succession of dominoes leading all the way to the Promised Land.

Take an inventory of your life today to see what is in your hand right now. It may be people, relationships, interests, opportunities, thoughts, or dreams. Chances are that the seeds of your future have already been sown into the soil of your life. Ask God to give you the wisdom to discern them; then have the diligence to water them and the patience to wait for the harvest.

Help Others Fulfill Their God-Given Vision

While you're waiting for God to bring about the fulfillment of your vision, or even if you don't yet know what God is calling you to do, put the law of sowing and reaping to work for you. Find someone else who has a vision from the Lord and invest into that person's vision as if it were your own. Volunteer your time, energy, and resources to push someone else forward. You will find that as you sow into someone else's vision, you will soon reap a vision of your own.

Be Faithful Wherever You Find Yourself

It used to be standard practice for large companies to "headhunt" talented executives from prestigious universities or other successful companies for senior positions. But more and more I have noticed that it is becoming the policy of many large companies to promote from within. They look for talented people from their own ranks, individuals who have proven their trustworthiness and worked their way up the ladder, even from very low positions. This has always been God's preferred method of promotion. God looks for faithful people He can promote and bless. He tests us with small tasks to see how we will react, and when we have proven ourselves, He gives us bigger responsibilities.

Moses had one of the most important leadership positions in history. He was assigned the challenging task of leading an entire nation—God's chosen people, no less—across the wilderness to the Promised Land. It's interesting to think that before God appointed Moses to such an important role, Moses had a similar assignment but on a much smaller scale. Rather than leading people through the wilderness, he was leading a flock of stinky sheep through that very same wilderness—for forty years! How could God have trusted Moses to lead His people if Moses had not proven His faithfulness leading sheep?

We see this principle articulated over and over in Jesus's teaching. In the parable of the talents Jesus says to the servant who had doubled his investment, "Well done, good and faithful servant! You have been faithful with a few things; I will put you in charge of many things" (Matt. 25:21, NIV). In another parable Jesus said, "Whoever can be trusted with very little can also be trusted with much, and whoever is dishonest with very little will also be dishonest with much" (Luke 16:10, NIV). He goes on to compare the servant's ability to handle money with his ability to handle "true riches": "So if you have not been trustworthy in handling worldly wealth, who will trust you with true riches? And if you have not been trustworthy with someone else's property, who will give you property of your own?" (Luke 16:11–12, NIV).

Psalm 75:6–7 says, "For promotion cometh neither from the east, nor from the west, nor from the south. But God is the judge: he putteth down one, and setteth up another." The scripture is clear: promotion does not come from the horizontal plane—the east or the west. That is to say that men are not the source of promotion. Also, promotion does not come from the south; the devil is also not the source of promotion. If promotion comes not from the south, east, or west, we know by process of elimination from which direction promotion comes—north! Look up! God is the promoter, and He promotes those who are faithful.

Chapter 19

WHAT IF I'VE BEEN WAITING
FOR A LONG TIME?

IN THIS CHAPTER I want to speak to two different groups of people: I want to address those who have been seeking God's will for a long time but have not yet discovered it, and I want to speak to those who feel they know what God's will is but have been waiting a long time to see it fulfilled.

First, for those of you who have been seeking God's will for a long time but have not discovered it, I have a challenge, a question, and an encouragement.

The Challenge: It is important to realize that there is a big difference between seeking God's will and just waiting for something to happen. The word *seek* implies action, not passivity. Those who are seeking God's will are actively asking for God's direction, looking for opportunities to serve, helping others fulfill their God-given visions, and being faithful wherever they find themselves at the moment (as we discussed in the previous chapter). You need to examine your heart in honesty before God and ask yourself, in light of these things, whether you are truly seeking God's will for your life or if you're just waiting for a "lucky break." There is a big difference. If you can honestly say you are actively seeking God's will as outlined above but still have not discovered it, there are two things I would say to you.

The Question: Is it possible that you have already discovered God's will for your life but have not been willing to recognize it as such? Sometimes people miss something that is right in front of them because what they are looking for does not appear the way they expected it to. Maybe you are looking for a big ministry and worldwide recognition, but instead the Lord wants you to work behind the scenes. Be open to the possibility that what God has for you might not look the way you expected it to and that's why you haven't found it yet. If this is the case, don't be discouraged. If you trust God and follow His will wherever it leads, you will find that in the end you will be much happier than if you had gotten what you originally wanted. Your Father knows best. If you are confident that you are not failing to recognize God's will, then let me encourage you to keep seeking with all your heart.

The Encouragement: If you are still actively seeking God's will for your life, don't become frustrated; just keep on seeking and you will surely find. Don't allow the enemy to plant seeds of discouragement or doubt in your heart. Just become more and more determined, and with childlike audacity keep seeking until you find.

> Sometimes people miss something that is right in front of them because what they are looking for does not appear the way they expected it to.

Recently I was out shopping with my kids at our local mall. We passed one particular store where my son knows there is an elaborate toy train set that he loves to play with. He asked me if he could play with it before we left the mall, and I agreed. A few minutes later he asked again and again and again and again. The entire time we were in the mall he asked incessantly until finally I stopped prolonging the inevitable and said, "OK, let's go play with the train." He was elated. As we were walking toward the store, he said, "Dad, I just keep asking because I *really* want to play with the train. Can I have a drink?" With one request granted, he was immediately on to the next one!

I know I am not the only parent who has a persistent child. They all seem to come with this built-in quality. But believe it or not, it does not annoy me. In fact, I think we could all learn from this. Jesus seemed to think so.

In Matthew 7:7–8 Jesus is teaching about asking, seeking, and knocking. But it is important to note that the Greek implies continued action, which is why the Amplified Bible translates the passage like this: *"Keep on asking and it will be given you; keep on seeking and you will find; keep on knocking* [reverently] and [the door] will be opened to you. For everyone who *keeps on asking* receives; and he who *keeps on seeking* finds; and to him who *keeps on knocking,* [the door] will be opened" (emphasis added).

Keep on asking. Keep on seeking. Keep on knocking. Keep on keeping on. It sounds a lot like my son asking to play with the train and asking for a drink and asking for, well, everything. Interestingly enough, in the next verse, Jesus says, "Or what man is there of you, if his son asks him for a loaf of bread, will he hand him a stone?" (v. 9, AMP). Here we see that Jesus uses this type of persistence in the context of exactly what a child would do.

One day it suddenly occurred to me: children are persistent because they have to be. They are dependent creatures. The younger they are, the more needy they are, and as such, in order to survive, they must master the skill of persistence. My son asks incessantly because he sees me as his source. If I don't give him water, he'll go thirsty. If I don't give him food, he'll starve. I am his source of shelter, of clothing, of protection, of recreation—of everything. He is persistent because he must be so to survive, and he has every right to be.

My son comes to me without hesitation or apprehension. He

asks with a righteous audacity. He is not discouraged or put off in the least when I don't immediately meet his request; he simply asks again. Each time he asks, he expects to receive just as the time before. His seeking is incredibly simple and trusting. I would say it is a wonderful example of faith.

But the older we become, the less willing people are to give us what we need simply for the asking. We must win our bread and climb the ladder of success. In order to survive, we must lose our dependency and master self-sufficiency. As we become self-reliant, we hate to ask for anything. We don't want to be pushy or presumptuous. If we must ask for something, we do so with timidity and are loath to ask a second time.

So many people make the mistake of approaching God with this dignified, grown-up demeanor. They make cautious but eloquent requests that are logical and reasonable. If they don't see an answer right away, they either assume it was not God's will and leave it at that, or they become offended, frustrated, and discouraged.

But the prize goes to the ones who are bold enough to take hold of heaven with reckless confidence. I am not talking about arrogant presumption but childlike assurance. Leave your incredible intellect, your proud rationale, and your deceptive self-reliance at the door. Come to terms with your utter and total dependency upon your Father. Understand that your sonship is the only grounds upon which you can approach God in the first place. As a son or daughter of God it is your righteous privilege to ask, and it is God's divine pleasure to answer. Therefore, ask with audacity, confidence, and persistence.

> If you trust God and follow His will wherever it leads, you will find that in the end you will be much happier than if you had gotten what you originally wanted.

Keep asking like a child asks a father for bread. Keep knocking as the widow before the unjust judge in Luke 18. Keep seeking as if seeking for a pearl of great price (Matt. 13:45–46). Push through resistance like the woman with the issue of blood (Mark 5:25–34). Lean into the Word like a man walking against the wind. Clamp down on His promises like a pit bull with a T-bone. Place a demand on what's yours. Give Him no rest day or night until His answer breaks through like a pent-up flood and makes your desert to blossom like a rose. If the answer doesn't come immediately, don't be discouraged or frustrated. With expectancy and trust just lift your eyes to the hills and ask and ask again. Keep on asking. Keep on seeking. Keep on knocking. Keep on keeping on until you receive—and you will in Jesus's name!

Don't Give Up

If you believe you already know what God's will is for your life, but you've been waiting a long time for it to be fulfilled, let me encourage you with these words from Habakkuk 2:2–4 where God told Habakkuk: "Write the vision and make it plain on tablets, that he may run who reads it. For the vision is yet for an appointed time; but at the end it will speak, and it will not lie. Though it tarries, wait for it; because it will surely come" (NKJV).

The important thing to remember is that you are planting seeds right now that will determine what you will reap tomorrow. Your attitude is a seed. Your time is a seed. Your prayers are seeds. One common reason people get frustrated is that they begin planting good seeds (such as the ones we discussed in the previous chapter about what to do while you are seeking God's will), yet they are not seeing the fruit they want. Let me explain it like this.

Some time ago I decided it was time to get back in shape. I bought a set of exercise videos that had come to me with high recommendations. The very first day of my new regimen, my six-year-old son and four-year-old daughter were joined by their mother who decided that they wanted to exercise with me. So the four of us were warming up together for an invigorating callisthenic workout. We were only about five minutes into the video—still somewhere in the stretches—when my son turned to me with great excitement and said, "Hey, Dad, look. You almost got muscles. Look at your elbows!"

My wife and I had a real good laugh, but my poor son never understood what was so funny. I didn't have the heart to break it to him that it doesn't work that way. It takes a long time and many doughnuts, followed by excessive periods of sedentary inactivity and lack of resolve to become as out of shape as I was. And getting fit, losing weight, and building muscle doesn't happen overnight either—much less after a few minutes of warming up. We don't live on a farm, so my son is learning the principles of sowing and reaping in other ways. Unfortunately these are principles many adults still do not understand.

When I was a pastor, a newly saved church member approached me after the service one Sunday morning. He was obviously disgruntled and wanted a word with me. "Pastor," he said, "the Bible says to 'test God' with the tithe and offering, and that's exactly what I did." He went on to explain that before he became a Christian and started attending the church, his family had been going through a season of great financial hardship. Now that he was learning about the Bible, he read Malachi's guarantee that the "windows of heaven" would be opened over those who give.

The past Sunday he decided to "test God." He emptied out his wallet in the offering plate and gave for the first time. But the subsequent week was not as he had anticipated. His financial difficulties continued, and he was concerned that there was something wrong with the Bible. He had sown a seed but had not reaped a harvest.

This brother's mistake was a basic misunderstanding of how sowing and reaping works, much like my son when he was examining my elbows for muscle sprouts five minutes into our first workout. I explained to this gentleman that whatever you are harvesting now is not the result of what you planted a few hours ago.

Today you are reaping what you planted months ago, even years ago, in a different season. Likewise the seeds you plant today won't necessarily be ready for harvest by the next day or even by next Sunday.

Imagine with me what it may have been like to grow up on an ancient Israeli farm. The long winter months have reduced the once-plentiful pantries to empty shelves, and the family is now living on meager rations and dreaming about a loaf of bread fresh from the oven. Suddenly the rain begins to pour, and the once-dusty fields are becoming rivers. The father says to his young son, "Come, it's time to sow." Together they walk out to the barn where the father climbs into the loft and pulls down huge bags of grain.

"Father!" the young boy exclaims, "now we can make bread!" The father replies, "No, my son. This grain is not for eating. Come, I will show you what it is for." He fills a sack with grain, and they wade into the flooded fields. Then the father does the most absurd thing; he begins throwing the grain into the water! That night at the dinner table, the little boy eats his paltry portion and wonders why his father threw all that grain away. Many weeks will go by before he understands, but one day the water will recede and the little boy will step outside and behold a miracle. The fields will be full of tiny sprouts, racing heavenward to produce a harvest of golden grain. It was this ancient farming technique that Solomon was referring to when he wrote, "Cast your bread upon the waters, for you will find it after many days" (Eccles. 11:1, NKJV).

Throwing perfectly good grain into the water when you are hungry is a difficult thing to do, but what is more difficult is waiting *many days* for the harvest. This is why Paul encourages us by saying, "Let us not be weary in well doing: for in *due season* we shall reap, if we faint not" (Gal. 6:9, emphasis added).

It is amazing and sobering to think that we are all planting seeds all the time. Sowing and reaping are not confined to putting money in an offering plate. That cheeseburger you ate, that movie you watched, that comment you made, that time you spent with your family, that book you read—everything you do is a seed that will produce a harvest (good or bad) in the future. Be careful what you plant in this season because you will eat it in the next.

In the end our lives are a sum total of the decisions we have made—a harvest, if you will, of what we have sown. You can't usually change today's harvest by sowing good seeds today, but if you will determine to sow the right seeds day in and day out, in "due season" you will reap your harvest if you "faint not."

If you have been waiting for a long time and still have not seen the fulfillment of God's promise for your life, keep sowing good seeds and beware of impatience. Allow God to do the work in your heart that He is trying to accomplish. The children of Israel walked in circles in the wilderness decade after decade because they did not learn their lesson. Some people keep going in circles because they never learn what God is trying to teach them, and they never move to the next phase because they never pass the test. Stop squirming and wiggling and trying to get through with this as quickly as possible, but be faithful and patient. When you pass the test, He will lead you forward.

Chapter 20

HOW DO I STAY IN THE WILL OF GOD?

AH, GREAT IT is to believe the dream as we stand in youth by the starry stream; but a greater thing is to fight life through and say at the end, the dream is true!"[1] Those are the words of the American poet Edwin Markham. A much wiser man, King Solomon, said it this way, "Better is the end of a thing than the beginning thereof" (Eccles. 7:8). It is a wonderful thing indeed to discover God's will, but a more wonderful thing to remain in it for the rest of your life and to say at the end, "I did the will of God."

When the apostle Paul came to the end of his life, after fulfilling God's plan, he was able to say with confidence and assurance, "The time of my departure is at hand. I have fought the good fight, I have finished the race, I have kept the faith. Finally, there is laid up for me the crown of righteousness, which the Lord, the righteous Judge, will give to me on that Day" (2 Tim. 4:6–8, NKJV). As we come to the end of this book, it is my sincere prayer that you will not only discover God's will, but that you will also one day hear those most anticipated words from the master, "Well done, My good and faithful servant."

It is heartbreaking to realize that not everyone who begins the race will finish it. There are often many casualties along the way.

As I sit writing this final chapter, I ask the Holy Spirit to help me to communicate to you a word that will help you to stay the course and to fulfill all that God has in store for your life.

Stand in Your Pea Patch

In 2 Samuel 23 we read about David's "mighty men," a small militia of extraordinarily skilled warriors. It was not a big army, but it was a tough army, like a highly trained special forces unit. They were amazingly proficient with their weapons. In fact, the Bible says they could split a hair with their slingshots—left-handed! (See 2 Chronicles 12:2.) The chapter goes on to describe in greater detail the exploits of a small handful within that group who were the best of the best of the best!

These men were like real-life superheroes who would make Rambo look like a Girl Scout. One of these men was Adino. "He lift up his spear against eight hundred, whom he slew at one time" (v. 8). "Abishai…lifted up his spear against three hundred, and slew them" (v. 18). Benaiah the son of Jehoiada "slew two lionlike men of Moab: he went down also and slew a lion in the midst of a pit in time of snow: and he slew an Egyptian, a goodly man: and the Egyptian had a spear in his hand; but he went down to him with a staff, and plucked the spear out the Egyptian's hand, and slew him with his own spear" (vv. 20–21). But my favorite one of David's mighty men was Shammah.

> Now after him was Shammah the son of Agee a Hararite. And the Philistines were gathered into a troop, where there was a plot of ground full of lentils, and the people fled from the Philistines. But he took his stand in the midst of the plot, defended it and struck the Philistines; and the LORD brought about a great victory.
>
> —2 SAMUEL 23:11–12, NAS

Some scholars believe Shammah, mentioned in 2 Samuel, could be the same man whom Judges 3:31 calls Shamgar, who killed six hundred Philistines with an ox goad! Either way one thing is clear: Shammah won an overwhelming victory against impossible odds, and through his courage and valor, God brought about a great triumph for Israel. Let us consider his story.

It was an ordinary day in Israel. The people were going about their daily business as usual. On the outskirts of the city, in a remote field, a group of laborers was harvesting a meager crop of peas. Suddenly a shadow fell on that pea patch from the hills as hundreds of Philistine soldiers appeared, armed in full battle gear. Fear struck the hearts of the people. These farmers were mere peasants, armed only with spades, hoes, and other agricultural tools. They knew they had no chance against a professional army. Remaining in that field would mean almost certain death. They looked down at their pea patch situated on an insignificant plot of land, and they realized that it was not worth risking life and limb to defend that ground. They dropped their farming tools and ran for their lives.

> If you are to go the distance and fulfill God's will for your life, you must have integrity, focus, and perseverance.

This would have been the end of the story, but unfortunately for the Philistines there was one man in the field that day who was not just a peasant or a farmer—he was a warrior. He was one of David's "mighty men." Shammah was perhaps one of the greatest warriors who has ever lived, and this was to be his most glorious battle. From the story of Shammah I would like to give you the three words of wisdom that I believe will help you to remain in the will of God. His story reveals three qualities that I believe are nonnegotiable if you are to go the distance and fulfill God's will for your life: integrity, focus, and perseverance.

Mind in the Beginning What Matters in the End

Unlike the untrained peasant farmers who had fled the field, Shammah understood something about the tactics of warfare. Maybe this field was nothing but an ordinary pea patch, but this attack was not random—it was highly strategic. Perhaps the Philistines had chosen this pea patch because they thought no one would bother to defend such a worthless field and they could take it without a battle. But on this piece of land the Philistines would establish a stronghold and a base of operations from which they could launch future attacks on the nation of Israel.

When the enemy comes to assault your life, he is not going to start with the thing you are most diligent over. He is going to attack your pea patch: that thing he figures you will not bother to defend and where he thinks you will compromise. And in that compromise he will establish a stronghold to take over your life. I'm sure you've seen this before.

A couple has just gotten married. They are so in love and can't spend enough time together. But a few years later a radical transformation has taken place. They hate each other and want a divorce. You ask, "How did this happen?" I'll tell you how it happened. It happened one pea patch at a time. Solomon wrote, "[It's] the little foxes that spoil the vines" (Song of Sol. 2:15, NKJV). A little bit of dishonesty here, a little bit of disrespect there, a hurtful word, a transgression unforgiven; soon a root of bitterness sets in, and before long the enemy has successfully established a stronghold in that couple's relationship. From that compromised zone he will continue to assault their marriage until he has razed it to the ground.

Having integrity means minding the small things—and being as vigilant over them as over the big things. Shammah was an experienced warrior. He knew that if he compromised this little pea patch, soon the enemy would be kicking down his front door. He was fiercely determined not to give up one inch to the Philistines. If we can defend even the smallest, most insignificant pea patches in our lives, the enemy will not be able to gain a foothold. Rather than seeing how close we can get to the cliff of sin without falling over, we should seek to avoid even the appearance of evil (1 Thess. 5:22).

Rather than asking, "How much compromise is too much?" we should be constantly aiming to raise our personal standards to be more like Jesus. Murder was condemned under the law, but Jesus said hatred is murder. Adultery was condemned under the law, but Jesus said lust is adultery. Jesus understood that murder grows from the seed of hatred, and adultery grows from the seed of lust. Once the seed has been planted, the tree, while not fully mature, has been born. It is much better to crush the seeds of sin before they are planted than to have to try to chop down a giant redwood of evil compulsions and addictions. Susanna Wesley gave this word of wisdom to young John Wesley: "If you would judge of the lawfulness or unlawfulness of pleasure, then take this simple rule: Whatever weakens your reason, impairs the tenderness of your conscience, obscures your sense of God, and takes off the relish of spiritual things—that to you is sin."[2]

Having integrity means being brutal with sin. When the Philistines invaded that pea patch, Shammah did not throw up his arms and say, "Come on, guys. Can we talk about this? Let's see if we can negotiate a mutually agreeable arrangement here." Shammah did not meet the Philistines with a white flag but with a sharpened ox goad. He hadn't come to talk but to fight. If we are to be men and women of integrity, it will not happen by accident. Integrity requires ferocity and resolve. We see this demonstrated in Job when he said, "Till I die I will not remove mine integrity from me. My righteousness I hold fast, and I will not let it go: my heart shall not reproach me so long as I live" (Job 27:5–6).

Having integrity means doing the right thing, even when it means standing alone. Shammah stood in that field all by himself. How he would have loved to stand back to back with one of his mighty comrades from David's militia, but they were not with him.

The peasant farmers had fled the scene and left Shammah without even moral support. He stood alone, yet he stood his ground.

Having integrity means doing the right thing even when no one is looking. Shammah didn't fight that battle with the Philistines because he wanted to be a celebrity warrior. The rest of the Israelites had left him alone. He was not fighting like a gladiator in a stadium before a crowd of cheering fans. Yet somehow, thousands of years later, we are still talking about his glorious battle. Somehow the word got out, and everyone heard about what happened in that obscure pea patch. Jesus said, "There is nothing concealed that will not be disclosed, or hidden that will not be made known. What you have said in the dark will be heard in the daylight, and what you have whispered in the ear in the inner rooms will be proclaimed from the roofs" (Luke 12:2–3, NIV). Character is who are you when no one is looking. That is the real you.

Most of the time character flaws hide below the surface invisible to the casual observer. People take great care to make sure no one sees their problems or shortcomings. But if not dealt with, these invisible infections mature into very public diseases.

Several years ago a high-profile preacher was involved in a very public scandal that caused great shame and pain for him and his family, ruined his ministry, and disgraced the body of Christ. After his illicit activity was revealed on national news, his congregation sat in shock and disbelief as he delivered an apology on Sunday morning that began like this: "I am so sorry. I am sorry for the disappointment, the betrayal, and the hurt. I am sorry for the horrible example I have set for you. I have an overwhelming, all-consuming sadness in my heart for the pain that you and I and my family have experienced over the past few days. I am so sorry for the circumstances that have caused shame and embarrassment to all of you."

How does a man, so mightily used by God, fall like this? It happens one pea patch at a time, one unprotected, seemingly insignificant area of life that is not consecrated to God at a time. A little compromise here, a lustful imagination there. Every concession seems so inconsequential. Sin begins as a cute little pet, but it grows into a beast that is never satisfied. As it is fed, it only becomes bigger and hungrier; gratification becomes more difficult, and soon the pet has become the master. In the end you will either kill the beast or it will kill you. The devil is very patient. He is willing to wait, sometimes for many years, while sin matures. Once the enemy has established a stronghold in someone's life, he will not stop until he has destroyed that person or until that person destroys the stronghold.

Imagine if this minister could have heard himself delivering that speech many years before this public scandal took place. Imagine if he could have looked into the future and seen himself on that fateful Sunday morning telling his tearful congregation, "I am a deceiver and a liar.... " Imagine if he could have seen the pain and the heartache that would grow from those small, early compromises. What if he could have seen the tears in his wife's and children's eyes? If he could have seen the end from the beginning, I think a righteous anger would have arisen in his soul, and he would have stood his ground and fought for every inch of territory.

I'll never forget a sermon I heard when I was in seminary from our college president, Michael L. Brown, PhD. He preached about a fascinating word that appears in the Hebrew Scriptures sixty-one times; it is *acharit* (pronounced *"a-kha-reet"*). There is really no single word equivalent for it in English, but the literal meaning of it is "the final or ultimate end." It speaks of the backside or hinder parts, the part that is to follow, the part that is to come, the final end.[3] We find this word used in Psalm 37:37–38: "Mark the perfect man, and behold the upright: for the end [*acharit*] of that man is peace. But the transgressors shall be destroyed together: the end [*acharit*] of the wicked shall be cut off."

The German monk Thomas à Kempis is well known to have said, "Happy is the man who hath the hour of his death always before his eyes."[4] But if he would have been Hebrew, he probably would have said it this way: "Happy is the man who hath the hour of his *acharit* [his final end] always before his eyes." This would have been a better quote anyway since there is a final end beyond the hour of our death and beyond the grave.

I heard someone say recently that he was shocked when he picked up the newspaper and found his own name in the obituary section. Apparently another guy in town had the same name as this gentleman. But when he saw his name among the deceased, it really made him think about the end of his own life. Imagine that you had the opportunity to write your own obituary. What would you put in it? How would you want it to read? Have you stopped to think about your *acharit*?

Evangelist Reinhard Bonnke once told me that as a young man, he was kneeling at the altar in a pastors' prayer meeting next to an elderly servant of God. He overheard the old man weeping as he asked God to please forgive him for the unclean things he had allowed into his life. This moved the young evangelist deeply. Reverend Bonnke said he moved away to another spot where no one could hear, and he cried out to God with a prayer of his own. "Lord," he said, "help me to mind in the beginning what matters in the end."

As I write this book, Evangelist Bonnke is seventy-two years of age and has never been involved in a scandal or a fall. I heard someone ask him once, "Is there anything in your life you would do differently?" "No," he said, "I have no regrets." What a wonderful example for the next generation!

Oh, my friend, may we purpose in our hearts to live life in such a way that we will not have to weep in the *acharit* over uncleanness and sin that we allowed into our lives. "I urge you," Paul said, "to live a life worthy of the calling you have received" (Eph. 4:1, NIV). Let us determine to live a life worthy of the calling, a life of integrity, minding in the beginning what matters in the end.

Don't Get Distracted

I think it is interesting that 2 Samuel 23:12 tells us exactly where Shammah strategically positioned himself. It says, "He stationed himself in the middle of the field" (NKJV). He wasn't standing out on the fringes, and he wasn't in one of the corners. He was right in the very center of the field. I have seen many people who were called to a particular field, but over the years they became distracted. They lost their focus and wandered to the fringes of their field and sometimes even drifted into other fields they were never called to serve. If you are going to remain in the center of God's will for your life, you must resolve to stand in the middle of the field to which He has called you and remain focused without allowing the enemy to distract you from that call.

Several years ago I preached in Madrid, Spain, in a stadium used for bullfights. Wanting to get the full cultural experience, the night before our campaign began, I went to see my first (and only) bullfight. I will never forget that experience because it became a powerful lesson for my life.

I witnessed the brutal death of half a dozen bulls that night. Most of them had been raised far from civilization and had rarely seen human beings before. Once they were released into the noisy chaos of the bullfighting arena, they began to get angry, looking around for a target to attack. There, in the middle of the arena, stood the matador. He began to wave his cape, and the bull flew into a rage.

Now you must understand that for the matador this is an extremely dangerous sport. These undomesticated bulls, essentially wild animals, are one-thousand-pound killing machines. They could easily trample, crush, or gorge the small, cape-waving man to death. But the bullfighter has a secret weapon—distraction.

The bull charges the matador over and over again, coming closer and closer to his opponent. But just when the bull is about to hit his target, suddenly another man rushes in from the side and stabs the bull with a lance and then runs away. The bull turns to see his surprise assailant and begins to move toward him when another man runs in from the opposite side and stabs him with another lance and runs away.

The lances dangle from the bull's thick hide. Although the stabs draw blood, they are far from mortal wounds—the bull is an extremely tough animal. But this peripheral assault serves a very important purpose. It effectively distracts the bull from his main target: the matador. If the bull could just stay focused on one target, he would almost certainly win every fight. But he is continually changing his target, going after one distraction and then another. What the bull doesn't realize is that he is in a race against time. The blood flowing out of the lance wounds begins to weaken him. Minute by minute the bull grows weaker, slower, and more faint. Finally he collapses in the sand, and this is when the matador moves in for the fatal blow.

Through the Holy Spirit we are equipped to live fruitful and effective lives, accomplishing all that God has for us to do. The devil is no match for the Spirit of God who lives within us. Greater is He who is in us than he that is in the world. But like the bullfighter, the enemy has a secret weapon—distraction. If the devil can't stop us, he will attempt to derail us with one distraction and then another. The devil knows something we so often forget—that we are in a race against time. As with the bull whose wounds are bleeding, time is running out for all of us. Every minute that we are distracted from what God has called us to do is a minute closer to the end of the fight. The devil will even use "good" things as distractions if he can to keep us from the best things that God has in store.

In James 4:14 our lives are described as "a vapour, that appeareth for a little time, and then vanisheth away." There are not enough hours in a day to do everything. There are not enough years in your life to live for everything. There is not enough blood in your veins to bleed for everything. That's why it is so important that you choose your battles wisely, don't get distracted and sacrifice what is "best" on the altar of what is "good."

In 1 Corinthians 9:24 Paul encourages us to run the race of our lives "in such a way that you may win" (NAS). A person who is running to win sets his eyes on the finish line and goes for it with all his might. A person who is running to win has made a choice to lay down everything else for the sake of the prize.

Reinhard Bonnke once told me the story of how a newspaper had spread vicious lies about him. His friends, jealous for his reputation, urged him to respond. But when he prayed, the Lord spoke to him and said, "You are My harvest worker. Don't stop the combine harvester just to catch a mouse!"

There are a lot of good battles out there to fight, and the devil would be happy if you would get involved in every one of them, because if he can keep you distracted chasing mice, he can rob you of your harvest. John Maxwell wrote, "At age sixty I now look back at my youth and I cringe at my naïveté. My toolbox of experience had only one tool in it: a hammer. If all you have is a hammer, everything looks like a nail. So I pounded and pounded. I fought many battles I shouldn't have."[5]

Years ago a friend of mine became fascinated with a particular doctrinal debate. Although it was an issue of little or no real-life consequence, he was so sure he was right that he started an ongoing argument within the church where he was on staff. The pastor, realizing that this debate was causing more harm than good, asked him to drop it. He refused, choosing rather to forfeit his job and ministry. This story would not be worth sharing if it were the only time I have seen this. But I could point to several people who are out of ministry today because they were derailed by something petty. Somehow they lost sight of the big harvest and started chasing mice.

Paul exhorts us to "avoid foolish controversies and genealogies and arguments and quarrels about the law, because these are unprofitable and useless" (Titus 3:9, NIV). Notice that Paul did not call these controversies, arguments, and quarrels sinful things; he called them unprofitable and useless things. Even if something is not necessarily a sin, it can still distract us from what is important. That is why Paul was exhorting us not to get distracted but to stay focused on what is useful and profitable.

I've seen pastors who spent more time doing construction projects at their church than they spent pastoring their people. I have seen ministries of evangelists whom God called to preach the gospel of salvation transform into humanitarian organizations. I have seen people who have been gifted in particular areas decide to follow more lucrative paths that took

> You can be extraordinarily gifted, talented, anointed, and blessed, but without persistence you will have little impact because the great victories are always on the other side of great battles.

them away from their calling. These are all examples of the ways the enemy can distract us from God's will for our lives. It's not that the distractions are necessarily bad things. In fact, sometimes they are wonderful things. But if they keep us from the best thing—doing God's will—the enemy has succeeded.

We've been talking a lot about God's will for your life, but remember, the devil also has a plan for you, and his plan is to make you ineffective and unfruitful. He would love for you to park your combine harvester to chase mice. If he cannot block you, he will try to derail you. He will try to distract you from your assignment. Ignore him. Keep you eyes on the prize, keep fighting in the middle of your field, and run your race in such a way that you will win!

Never Give Up

When Shammah made his stand in the middle of that pea patch, he was not hanging around just to get a few licks in before making an exit. For Shammah there were only two options: win or die! He stood his ground, he defended that pea patch, and 2 Samuel 23:12 tells us about the happy ending: "The LORD wrought a great victory."

We all want to discover God's will for our lives, but once we discover it, that is not the end; it is only the beginning! Once you have your assignment from God, then you have to stand in your field and fight until God gives the victory. This requires a quality that few seem to possess—perseverance.

In Ephesians 6 we are commanded to "put on the whole armour of God" (v. 11). But verses 13 and 14 say something important: "And having done all, to stand. Stand therefore." In other words, after you have made all the preparation to stand, now there is one thing left to do—stand! This is where many people miss it. They go to great lengths to discover God's will for their lives. They go to Bible college; they read books; they receive prophetic words; they prepare themselves in every way possible. But when their skin begins to burn with the heat of the battle, they drop their weapons and retreat. I am aware that this is not a "feel-good" message.

We are always looking for shortcuts, tips, and tricks, but I'm afraid there is no way around this principle. You can be extraordinarily gifted, talented, anointed, and blessed, but without persistence you will have little impact because the great victories are always on the other side of great battles. The word *persevere* is made of the prefix *per*, which means "through," and *severe*. Victory comes to those who press through severe battles to the other side without quitting.

R. Alec Mackenzie, who wrote extensively on the subject of time management, said, "The ability to concentrate—to persevere on a course without distraction or diversion—is a power that has enabled men of moderate capability to reach heights of attainment that have eluded the genius. They have no secret formula other than to persevere."[6]

Helen Hayes won many prestigious awards during her acting career, which spanned nearly seventy years. But she attributed her success not to talent or ability: "Nothing is any good without endurance."[7] Chemist Louis Pasteur, who developed the disease-preventing process that came to be called pasteurization, said, "My strength lies solely in my tenacity."[8]

Apparently Shammah was not the only one of David's mighty men who knew what it meant to be persistent. The Bible says Eleazar fought so long and so hard in one battle that his hand froze to the sword (2 Sam. 23:10). When it comes to fulfilling God's will for your life, perseverance is not an option; it is an imperative. If Eleazar or Shammah would have let go of their swords or stopped fighting, the enemy would have killed them. If you let go of God's calling, you will never fulfill it.

What do you do when the going gets tough? Stand firm and don't let go! What do you do when the enemy begins to assail from all directions? Stand firm and don't let go! What do you do when you face financial difficulty, health problems, betrayal, abandonment, rejection, and pain? Stand firm and don't let go! My friend, the battle belongs to the Lord, and He will win it in His time. Our part is not to question; our part is to obey and stand firm until God gives the victory.

May we stand in our respective fields as David's mighty men did, prepared to fight to the death for God's kingdom. And when the day comes for us to leave this world, I pray that the sword will have to be pried out of our lifeless fingers. At the end may we not be found sitting in front of a television, but may we be found with our boots strapped on in the field where God has assigned us. Never give up! Never retreat! Never surrender to the enemy! Your fulfillment of God's will for your life is not only about you. It's about your children and your grandchildren and the future of God's eternal kingdom. So stand! Fight! And endure until the end. And God will give you the victory in Jesus's name!

~~The End~~

The Beginning...

Scan QR code

or visit
LiveBeforeYouDieBook.com/conclusion

NOTES

INTRODUCTION

1. *U.S. Army Space Reference Text* (Fort Leavenworth, KS: US Army Space Institute, 1993) http://www.fas.org/spp/military/docops/army/ref_text/chap6im.htm (accessed August 15, 2012).

2. National Weather Service, "Layers of the Atmosphere," http://www.srh.noaa.gov/jetstream/atmos/layers.htm (accessed August 15, 2012).

CHAPTER 1
DOES GOD REALLY HAVE A PLAN FOR MY LIFE?

1. As quoted in Greg Ogden, *Discipleship Essentials* (Downers Grove, IL: InterVarsity Press, 1998).

2. Healthsolution.in, "You Use 200 Muscles to Take One Step," http://tinyurl.com/7s5y89g (accessed March 21, 2012).

3. Emmett L. Williams and George Mulfinger Jr., *Physical Science for Christian Schools* (Greenville, SC: Bob Jones University Press, 1974), 628; Scott M. Huse, *The Collapse of Evolution* (Grand Rapids, MI: Baker Books, 1997).

4. Deane B. Judd and Günter Wyszecki, *Color in Business, Science and Industry—Wiley Series in Pure and Applied Optics*, Third Edition (New York: Wiley-Interscience, 1975), 388.

5. Howard Crosby Warren, *Human Psychology* (New York: Cornell University Library, 2009), 167.

6. Charles Darwin, *The Origin of Species: 150th Anniversary Edition* (New York: Penguin, 2003).

7. Lucille Keir, Barbara A. Wise, Connie Krebs, and Cathy Kelley-Arney, *Medical Assisting: Administrative and Clinical Competencies*, Sixth edition (Australia: Cenage Learning, 2007), 377.

8. David G. Myers, *Psychology*, 4th edition (New York: Worth Publishers Inc, 1995), 43.

9. Tim LaHaye and David Noebel, *Mind Siege* (Nashville: Word Publishing, 2000), 45.

10. Scott Lafee, "Wellnews: All the News That's Fit," *U-T San Diego*, July 31, 2007, http://www.utsandiego.com/uniontrib /20070731/news_lz1c31wellnuz.html (accessed August 16, 2012).

11. Sandra Aamodt and Sam Wang, *Welcome to Your Brain* (New York: Bloomsburg, 2008).

12. *Unlocking the Mystery of Life*, directed by Lad Allen (La Mirada, CA: Illustra Media, 2010), DVD.

13. Mark Eastman and Chuck Missler, *The Creator Beyond Time and Space* (Costa Mesa: CA: TWFT Publishers, 1996), 84.

CHAPTER 2
HAVE I MISUNDERSTOOD GOD'S WILL?

1. Darrell L. Bock, *Jesus According to Scripture* (Grand Rapids, MI: Baker Academic, 1990).

2. Mark Martin, "The Secret to David Green's Successful 'Hobby,'" CBN News, November 6, 2010, http://www.cbn .com/cbnnews/finance/2010/November/The-Secret-to-David -Greens-Successful-Hobby/ (accessed October 24, 2012).

3. ChristiaNet.com, "Hobby Lobby CEO, David Green," http:// christiannews.christianet.com/1096289115.htm (accessed August 21, 2012).

4. "Interview With Winifred Wentland CfaN's Field Director," http://www.bonnke.net/cfan/en/interviewww (accessed August 21, 2012).

CHAPTER 3
HOW DO I RECOGNIZE GOD'S WILL?

1. "His Plan for Me," author unknown. As quoted in Jill Briscoe *8 Choices That Will Change a Woman's Life* (New York: Howard Books, 2004), 198.

2. Ken Ham, *The New Answers Book 3* (Green Forest, AR: New Leaf Publishing Group/Master Books, 2010).

3. Kathryn Kuhlman in a sermon posted on YouTube, December 25, 2006, http://www.youtube.com/watch?v=xBpldBh346w (accessed August 21, 2012).

CHAPTER 4
WHAT IF GOD CALLS ME TO DO
SOMETHING I DON'T WANT TO DO?

1. "Jesus, Use Me" by Billy Campbell, Herb Smith, and Jack Campbell. Copyright © 1951 Gospel Publishing House. Admin. The Lorenz Corporation. International Copyright Secured. All Rights Reserved. Used by Permission.

CHAPTER 6
SECRET #1—THE KINGDOM COMES FIRST

1. Kathryn Kuhlman and Jamie Buckingham, *A Glimpse Into Glory* (Alachua, FL: Bridge-Logos, 1983). Viewed at Google Books.

2. Reinhard Bonnke, *Living a Life of Fire* (Orlando, FL: E-R Productions LLC, 2010), 246.

3. Paul Lee Tan, *Encyclopedia of 7700 Illustrations* (Rockville, Maryland: Assurance Publishers, 1984), 1208.

4. Mission Aviation Fellowship, "Nate Saint," http://www.maf .org/about/history/nate-saint#.UDTsDKllRqM (accessed August 22, 2012).

5. Kendra Cherry, "Hierarchy of Needs: The Five Levels of Maslow's Hierarchy of Needs," http://psychology.about.com/ od/theoriesofpersonality/a/hierarchyneeds.htm (accessed August 22, 2012).

CHAPTER 7
SECRET #2—THE SURRENDERED WILL

1. A. W. Tozer, *The Pursuit of God* (Radford, VA: Wilder Publications, LLC., 2008), 21.

2. *The Very Best of Winds of Worship* (Double CD), copyright © 1998 Vineyard Music Group, "More Love, More Power" is dedicated to the memory of John Wimber (1934–1997), http:// www.worship.co.za/series/mla-01.asp (accessed August 22, 2012).

CHAPTER 8
SECRET #3—HEARING GOD'S VOICE

1. Reinhard Bonnke and George Canty, *Holy Spirit Revelation and Revolution* (Orlando, FL: E-R Productions LLC, 2007), 59.

2. C. R. Lovell, *Plants and the Skin* (Oxford: Blackwell Scientific Publications, 1993).

3. François Fénelon, *The Seeking Heart*, as quoted by Fred Smith in "Leader's Insight: How Integrity Grows," *Leadership Journal*, October 15, 2007, http://www.christianitytoday .com/le/channel/utilities/print.html?type=collection&id=11655 (accessed August 22, 2012).

CHAPTER 10
SECRET #5—TAKE ACTION!

1. Jack Canfield, *The Success Principles* (New York: HarperCollins Publishers, 2005), 102–103.

CHAPTER 11
ENEMY #1—THE BANDIT OF LAZINESS

1. Hara Estroff Marano, "Procrastination: Ten Things to Know," *Psychology Today*, August 23, 2003, http://www .psychologytoday.com/articles/200308/procrastination-ten -things-know (accessed August 22, 2012).

2. "The Procrastinator's Poem" by unknown author, as quoted in *Sermons Illustrated*, BibleStudyTools.com, http://www .biblestudytools.com/pastor-resources/illustrations/ procrastination-11566723.html (accessed August 22, 2012).

CHAPTER 12
ENEMY #2—THE CEMETERY OF FEAR

1. Mack Tomlinson, *In Light of Eternity: The Life of Leonard Ravenhill* (Conway, AR: Free Grace Press, 2010).

CHAPTER 15
ENEMY #5—THE WITCHCRAFT OF REBELLION

1. "Trust and Obey" by John H. Sammis. Public domain.

2. Paul Washer, "A Sermon That Has Angered Many—Examine Yourself," preached at Grace Community Church in San Antonio, Texas, http://media.sermonaudio.com/mediapdf/5220621750.pdf (accessed August 24, 2012).

3. As quoted by Charles Stanley in "When the Odds Are Against You," In Touch With Charles Stanley, posted at LightSource .com, http://www.lightsource.com/devotionals/in-touch-with -charles-stanley/in-touch-feb-9-2010-11625982-11625982.html (accessed August 24, 2012).

CHAPTER 16
IF I ENCOUNTER RESISTANCE, AM I OUT OF GOD'S WILL?

1. Douglas Malloch, "Good Timber" as quoted in Al Bryant *Sourcebook of Poetry* (Grand Rapids, MI: Zondervan Publishing House, 1968), 456.

CHAPTER 18
WHAT SHOULD I DO WHILE I'M SEEKING GOD'S WILL?

1. Daniel Kolenda, *Your Kingdom Come* (Orlando, FL: E-R Productions, 2011), 36–39.

CHAPTER 20
HOW DO I STAY IN THE WILL OF GOD?

1. Edwin Markham quotes, ThinkExist.com, http://thinkexist
.com/quotation/ah-great_it_is_to_believe_the_dream_as_we_
stand/262707.html (accessed August 24, 2012).

2. Susanna Wesley as quoted in *Resource*, July/August 1990,
http://www.sermonillustrations.com/a-z/w/wesley_john.htm
(accessed August 24, 2012).

3. Michael L. Brown, *Go and Sin No More: A Call to Holiness*
(Ventura, CA: Regal, 2000).

4. Thomas à Kempis, *The Imitation of Christ*, Project Guten-
berg, http://www.gutenberg.org/cache/epub/1653/pg1653.html
(accessed August 24, 2012).

5. John Maxwell, *Leadership Gold: Lessons Learned From a Lifetime of Leading* (Nashville, TN: Thomas Nelson, 2008).

6. R. Alec Mackenzie, *The Time Trap* (New York: McGraw-Hill
Book Company, 1975).

7. As quoted by John Marks Templeton in *Worldwide Laws of
Life: 200 Eternal Spiritual Principles* (Radnor, PA: Templeton
Foundation Press, 1997).

8. Louis Pasteur quotes, ThinkExist.com, http://thinkexist.com/
quotes/louis_pasteur/ (accessed August 24, 2012).

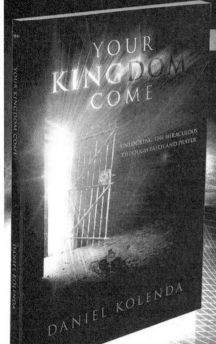

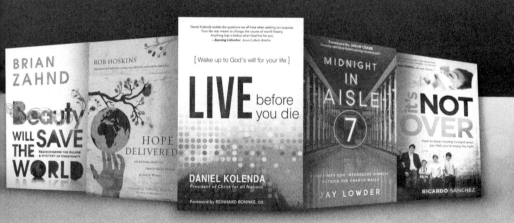

FREE NEWSLETTERS
TO HELP EMPOWER YOUR LIFE

Why subscribe today?

❑ **DELIVERED DIRECTLY TO YOU.** All you have to do is open your inbox and read.

❑ **EXCLUSIVE CONTENT.** We cover the news overlooked by the mainstream press.

❑ **STAY CURRENT.** Find the latest court rulings, revivals, and cultural trends.

❑ **UPDATE OTHERS.** Easy to forward to friends and family with the click of your mouse.

CHOOSE THE E-NEWSLETTER THAT INTERESTS YOU MOST:

- Christian news
- Daily devotionals
- Spiritual empowerment
- And much, much more

SIGN UP AT: **http://freenewsletters.charismamag.com**

8178